FOLK Shawls

25 knitting patterns

and tales from around the world

Cheryl Oberle

INTERWEAVE PRESS

Editor, Judith Durant
Technical editor, Dorothy T. Ratigan
Photography, Joe Coca
Illustration, Gayle Ford
Lino-cuts, Gary Oberle
Cover design, Bren Frisch
Production, Dean Howes
Author photo, Timothy M. Basgall

Interweave Press
201 East Fourth Street
Loveland, Colorado 80537
USA

Printed in China by Midas Printing International

Library of Congress Cataloging-in-Publication Data

Oberle, Cheryl, 1955–
    Folk shawls: 25 knitting patterns and tales from around the world/Cheryl Oberle.
        p. cm.
     Includes bibliographical references and index.
     ISBN 1-883010-59-4
        1.Shawls. 2.Knitting—Patterns. I. Title.

    TT825 .24 2000
    746.43'20432—dc21

                                                            99-058836

First printing: IWP—10M:1299:CC

To Gary Andrew Oberle,
my husband and my friend, this book is gratefully dedicated.

Acknowledgements

A book such as this is the work of many hands, and I thank those who taught me to love and appreciate the work of the hands in all its different and wonderful forms.

Many thanks to my test knitters, Lynn Gates, Anne Reed, Amy Rene Denio, Joan Knickerbocker, Allyssa Lyon, Linda Lutz, Sharon Jacobs, and Mary Kay McDermott. Your nimble fingers and diligent eyes are much appreciated.

All my gratitude to Judith Durant for being both editor and friend extraodinaire.

I am greatly obliged to Jillian Moreno who has told me for years that I should do a book of shawls. Look, Jillian, I did it!

Thanks to Dot Ratigan for being such a thorough and talented technical editor.

Thanks, too, to everyone on the production staff at Interweave Press whose expert work and attention to detail have made this process a pleasure. My gratitude goes to Linda Ligon for giving *Folk Shawls* a chance long before the current shawl craze was a reality.

I am indebted to Joe Coca and Timothy Basgall for their great photography and patient ways.

For generously supplying yarns, thanks to Meg Swansen of Schoolhouse Press, Marilyn King of Black Water Abbey Yarns, and Joe Coller of Baabaajoes Wool Company.

I am eternally grateful to Elizabeth Zimmermann and Barbara Walker; where would we be without you? To Medrith Glover and Karen Yaksick, thanks for creating the beautiful and inspiring "Graceful" and to Emily Ocker, a big thanks for permission to include her circular start.

Thanks as well, to Rain Olympia Crow, Marilyn Van Keppel, Ann Budd, Nancy Monzo, Liz Pfiefer, Emily Kirby, Barbara Thacker, Roxana Bartlett, and all of the folks at Shuttle, Spindles and Skeins for their inspiration, encouragement and support.

Love and gratitude go to Gary Oberle for his wonderful lino-cuts, his constant encouragement, the head-clearing Harley rides, and for helping me keep chaos at bay on the home front while I was writing this book.

To Jane Goughnour, my mother, thank you for showing me how to knit in the first place.

And last but not least, thanks to all my knitting students who over the years have kept me searching for beautiful things to bring back to them. This book was written for you.

Contents

Introduction

Of all the animals on Earth, only human beings wear clothes. Clothing is an expression of our beliefs, our dreams. and our creativity. What we wear represents to the world and to ourselves not only our physical circumstances, but also our emotional and spiritual states. We dress for the occasion and we relate to each other through the fabric we drape on our bodies.

Fabric is an ancient invention, a tool as necessary to survival as fire and as integral to our evolution as the wheel. Making fabric has given millions of people an opportunity to be creative. Knitted fabric is a simple fabric to make; what could be more elegantly elementary than creating fabric by hand using only yarn and two needles? It's also imminently portable during production. Knitted garments are warm and flexible. The tendency of knitting to drape and cling to the form makes even a simple knitted rectangle a versatile garment—it is a stole to keep the shoulders warm, a scarf to protect the head, a blanket in which to wrap a baby, or a pouch to carry goods.

The shawl is perhaps the oldest of garments; whether knitted or woven it has been worn for centuries. The shawl appears in some guise and shape in many diverse cultures. Wherever people have been working, living, telling stories, and celebrating, there have been people wearing shawls, wrapped in blankets, draped in lace. Shawls are used for prayer and for mourning. Shawls are bridal veils and christening garments. Shawls bring comfort and drama to our lives.

This book is one of shawl patterns and traditions. Some of the shawls are taken directly from examples of knitted shawls and some are translated into knitting from other media such as weaving or lace making. There are twenty-five shawl patterns, along with historical and cultural information and a good old fairy tale or two. The patterns are designed for ease and enjoyment of knitting as well as wearing.

Shawls are not just a thing of the past—they are worn today around the world. Shawls are being rediscovered by haute couture; there is nothing like a shawl to add drama and individuality to an outfit. Wear a shawl, with silk or with denim, and you have wrapped yourself in an ancient and wonderful tradition. To those who say "I don't wear shawls" my answer is "That's because you haven't met the right shawl!" I hope you'll find it here.

Knitting, like prayer, is meditative and calming. The Vesper Bell *by Rudolf Eickemeyer, Jr. Collection of The Hudson River Museum, 75.29.64. Reprinted with permission.*

Knitted shawls are often part of the most important rites of passage.
L'Espagne by Edouard Boubat, 1955. Reprinted with permission.

One

Techniques

GENERAL SHAPES

The shawls in this book are square, rectangular, or triangular. These are common and popular shapes in many cultures because they can be worn in many ways.

Triangular shawls start in a variety of ways. Some start at the point and increase up to the top edge; some start at the center of the top edge and increase (yes, increase!) down to the point; and some start on the long outer edge with several hundred stitches and decrease up to the center of the top edge.

Square shawls also start in a variety of ways. Some begin in the center with a wonderfully easy and beautiful circular start; some start as a small central square with two borders worked on the outside; and some start on one side and are worked as a simple square.

Rectangular shawls are the simplest shapes and are started either on a long edge or from a short end.

CHOOSING YARNS

The yarn used for each model shawl is identified in the pattern. Using a similar yarn in the same weight will create a shawl very like the one shown. Using a yarn with a different gauge will change the size and effect of a shawl, but such changes are by no means to be avoided. Knitting a Faroese shawl in a sportweight yarn instead of the more traditional Shetland jumper weight or Icelandic laceweight creates a large dramatic wrap, lovely to look at and delicious to wear. Worsted weight will be even more sensational. When substituting yarn, be sure to buy the same yardage as specified in the pattern. Substituting by weight is not as accurate because yarn weights vary by gauge and fiber content. Be sure to make a swatch to determine that the knitted fabric feels and looks good. Shawls are wonderfully forgiving in terms of gauge and fit, but doing a gauge swatch helps you ascertain that the knitting is not too stiff or too loose. Animal and plant fibers block well, holding the shape they

are blocked to and thereby making the most of lace patterns. Synthetic fibers tend to creep back to the shape they had before blocking, which can obscure lace patterns.

NEEDLES AND EQUIPMENT

Needles

Many shawls can be knitted on either straight or circular needles, but some shawls are knitted in the round and require circular needles. Using a circular needle to knit a flat shawl back and forth helps distribute the weight into your lap rather than on one side or the other—thus the knitting is easier and less tiring. It is also helpful to have the length of cable on the circular needle to spread out the stitches and look at the pattern.

When knitting lace patterns, choose a needle with sharp points. Needles with rounded points don't "dig in" to the stitches well, making decreases difficult to work.

Markers

Markers are a great help when you're working with a large number of stitches. Placing a marker every fifty stitches while casting on eliminates counting over and over to be sure you've cast on the correct number. Placing a marker every few repeats in a long row of lace pattern helps you avoid overlooking a mistake until many stitches or rows later.

Swatching

Many shawls in this book require only a stockinette- or garter-stitch swatch. Some shawls require a swatch in the lace pattern. I recommend doing a swatch of the lace pattern to make sure that you find the lace interesting and enjoyable to knit. Cast on as close to thirty stitches as the pattern allows. For example, if the lace pattern has a multiple of ten plus six stitches, cast on twenty-six (two times ten plus six). Knit at least three inches. Once you've knitted the swatch, it is important to block it to get an accurate measurement. Shawls are usually stretched when they are blocked, so stretch the swatch for a correct measurement. Measure the entire width of the swatch and divide the measurement into the number of cast-on stitches. Doing a swatch helps you avoid any funny surprises that may otherwise wait down the road.

CASTING ON

When you're casting on for a shawl, be sure to do so loosely. Too-tight casting on can result in edges that roll and shawls that cup in uncomfortable and unattractive ways. Any cast-on can work well if done on a much larger needle than you'll be knitting with or on two of the needles you will be using held together as one. Some other good options, specified in some of the patterns, are listed below.

Cable Cast-On

This technique provides a flexible, strong, and attractive edge. Begin by making a slipknot and placing it on a needle held in your left hand. Insert the right needle into the slipknot and pull a loop through and place it on the left needle. *Insert the right needle between the two stitches (figure 1), yarn over the needle and pull a loop through (figure 2), put loop on left needle (figure 3). Repeat from *.

Be sure to put the right-hand needle back between the last two stitches before you tighten the yarn. This step increases flexibility and makes the edge look even without your having to pull the stitches too tight.

Invisible Cast-Ons

The-crochet-over-the-needle or the crochet-chain methods are the easiest to work with. Simply casting on and knitting a few rows of scrap yarn works well too.

Crochet-over-the-needle invisible cast-on

Make a slip knot and place it on a crochet hook. Hold the yarn in the left hand and the hook in the right hand. Hold a needle on top of the long strand of yarn in the left hand. *With hook, draw a loop over needle and through the slipknot (figure 1). You will now have pulled the yarn over the knitting needle and cast on a stitch. Place the yarn behind the knitting needle (figure 2) and repeat from * until you have the required number of stitches on the needle. With the last loop still on the crochet hook, cut the yarn and slip the tail through the loop on the hook. Pull up loosely. When you're ready

figure 1

figure 2

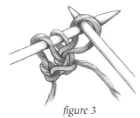

figure 3

Cable Cast-on

to take out the cast-on, pull the tail out of the last loop and pull on it to unchain the cast-on edge.

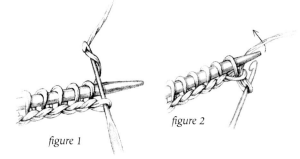

figure 1

figure 2

Crochet-over-the-needle invisible cast-on

Crochet-chain invisible cast-on

With a size F or G crochet hook and contrasting color scrap yarn, crochet a chain of as many loops as you will need stitches plus one. Do not break yarn. (If you need more stitches when you reach the end of your chain, simply crochet more.) With your main color yarn and beginning close to the first chain stitch, work from right to left, knitting up one stitch in each bump from the back of the chain. Do not knit into the smooth V shapes on the front of the chain or you will not be able to "unzip" the chain when you are ready to use the stitches. (But if you miss and knit into the wrong place, don't panic; the chain can later be surgically removed.)

Crochet-chain invisible cast-on

Knit up enough stitches for the desired number of pattern repeats. Excess crochet chains can be left hanging until the cast-on is removed.

When you're ready to remove the cast-on, slip the tail out of the last loop and pull on it to unchain the edge.

MODIFIED CIRCULAR START

This method is a modification of and was inspired by Emily Ocker's Circular Start. Use it for center-start shawls; it makes working on double-pointed needles and few stitches much easier. It also produces a beautiful center. Wooden or bamboo double-pointed needles are highly recommended because they do not slip out or flip around as much as the heavier metal needles.

Leaving a tail, make a large loop with the yarn. Hold the loop so that the crossing area of the loop is on the top and the tail is off to the left. With a double-pointed knitting needle, *reach inside the loop and pull the yarn coming from the ball through to make a stitch, then take the needle up over the top of the loop and yarn over;

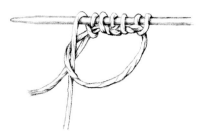

Modified Circular Start

repeat from * until you have the desired number of stitches on the needle. Turn and knit one row. If you're casting on an even number of stitches, the sequence ends with a yarnover and it will be difficult to keep from losing the last stitch. To solve this, pick up one extra stitch from the inside and then work these last two stitches together on the first row to get back to an even number of stitches. Divide the stitches evenly onto four double-pointed needles.

After working several rows of the shawl, pull on the tail to close the loop and draw the stitch up into a perfect little center.

JOINING NEW YARN

Joining a new ball of yarn can be tricky when knitting lace—it's difficult to weave loose ends into a lace pattern invisibly. When knitting with wool, I recommend making a felted join. Fray about two inches of both the old and the new yarn and overlap the frayed ends. Wash your hands to keep from soiling the yarn, and leave a little water on your palms. With the overlapped ends between your hands, vigorously rub the joined area, felting the ends together and creating one continuous length of yarn. Gently tug on the join to make sure it is secure. *Note:* This will not work with a superwash wool—the ends will not stay felted after blocking.

BINDING OFF

It is essential that you bind off your shawl stitches loosely to produce a flexible, non-constricted edge. As with casting on, this can be achieved by using two needles held together as one while working your chosen method. Alternatively, try Elizabeth Zimmermann's method, outlined below.

ELIZABETH ZIMMERMANN'S CASTING-ON CASTING-OFF METHOD

Break the yarn with right side facing and yarn coming off the left of the work. Thread the end through a tapestry needle. Working from left to right, *keep working yarn above and go into second stitch from front to back and then first stitch from back to front. Pull yarn

Elizabeth Zimmermann's Casting-On Casting-Off Method

through both stitches and slip first stitch off the needle. Repeat from *.

READING PATTERNS AND CHARTS

When following written instructions, it helps to write out each row on a separate 3" × 5" index card. Keeping the cards in order, punch a hole in the top corner and put the cards on a metal ring. Now when one row is finished, simply flip that card over and begin the next row from the next card. Use a paper clip on the top card to mark the current row so you don't lose your place if you are interrupted.

Knitting charts are read from bottom to top, and right-side (odd-numbered) rows are read from right to left while wrong-side (even-numbered) rows are read from left to right.

A magnetic board helps you keep track of charted pattern rows. Originally designed for counted cross-stitch, these boards are great for knitters. Put the chart on the board and place a magnetic strip directly above the row being worked. Move the magnet up as each row is completed. Post-its work too, and can be used to keep notes with your chart as well.

INCREASES

Kfb Knit into front and back of same stitch, making two stitches out of one.

Backward Loop Make One Make a snug backward loop onto the right-hand needle.

Backward Loop Make One

knit stitches right under the needle. Hold the two sets of stitches with right sides facing out.

Set-up: Bring the tapestry needle through the first stitch on the front needle purlwise and leave the stitch on the needle. Then bring the tapestry needle through the first stitch on the back needle purlwise and leave that stitch on the needle.

YARNOVERS

Believe it or not, there is a correct way to do yarnovers. If a knit stitch has just been completed, bring the yarn forward (from back to front) between the needles. If a purl stitch has just been completed, leave the yarn where it is, in front of the work. To knit the next stitch(es), bring the yarn over the top of the right-hand needle from front to back and proceed. To purl the next stitch(es), bring the yarn over the top of the right-hand needle from front to back and then under the needle from back to front (completely around the right-hand needle) and proceed.

DECREASES

Ssk Slip two stitches individually to right needle knitwise, slip left needle through front of stitches, knit two together through back loops.
K2tog knit two stitches together.
Sl 1, k2tog, psso slip one knitwise, knit two stitches together, pass slipped stitch over.
Sl 2, k1, p2sso slip two stitches together knitwise, knit 1, pass two slipped stitches over.

KITCHNER STITCH GRAFTING

Grafting Garter Stitch For the garter-stitch pattern to be continuous, the front piece must have purl bumps right under the needle, and the back piece must have

Grafting Garter Stitch

Step 1: Bring the tapestry needle through the same stitch on the front needle knitwise and slip the stitch off the needle. Bring the tapestry needle through the next stitch on the front needle purlwise and leave the stitch on the needle.

Step 2: Bring the tapestry needle through the same stitch on the back needle knitwise and slip the stitch off the needle. Bring the tapestry needle through the next stitch on the back needle purlwise and leave the stitch on the needle.

Repeat Steps 1 and 2 until no stitches remain on the needles, taking care to keep the tension of the grafting yarn the same as that of the knitting.

Grafting Stockinette Stitch Hold the two sets of stitches with right sides facing out.

Set-up: Bring the tapestry needle through the first stitch on the front needle purlwise and leave the stitch on the needle. Then bring the tapestry needle through the first stitch on the back needle knitwise and leave that stitch on the needle.

Step 1: Bring the tapestry needle through the same stitch on the front needle knitwise and slip the stitch off the needle. Bring the tapestry needle through the next stitch on the front needle purlwise and leave the stitch on the needle.

Step 2: Bring the tapestry needle through the same stitch on the back needle purlwise and slip the stitch off the needle. Bring the tapestry needle through the next stitch on the back needle knitwise and leave the stitch on the needle.

Repeat Steps 1 and 2 until no stitches remain on the needles, taking care to keep the tension of the grafting yarn the same as that of the knitting.

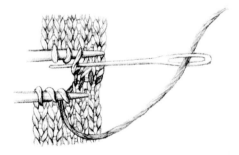

Grafting Stockinette Stitch

KNITTED-ON BORDERS

Several of the shawls presented here have borders that are attached to the outer edges as they are knitted. This method is preferable to knitting the borders separately and sewing them on because the sewing can constrict the edge, and make it inflexible. When attaching a border to "live" stitches of an outer edge, you attach the border every other row by working a stitch of the border together with a shawl stitch. The stitches may be worked by k2tog, ssk, or sl 1, k1, psso—just choose one method and be consistent.

You may also knit a border onto a shawl that does not have "live" stitches at the outer edge. Use the technique outlined at right to pick up stitches for the border.

There are two ways to work corners presented in the patterns. One is to attach several rows of the border to the same stitch(es). This provides enough ease for the border to form a pointed, rather than a rounded, corner. This method is used for the Fir Cone Square Shawl (page 83) and the Highland Triangle Shawl (page 88). The other method is to skip the last stitch of the border at the corners, creating short rows. This method is used for the Domovoi Shawl (page 77).

Lace borders often have a different number of stitches from row to row. Increasing and decreasing stitches creates the shaping and points of a border. I recommend counting the stitches in each pattern row before beginning the row so you'll know how many you should end up with at the end of that row. A yarnover will either make up for a decrease or act as an increase. When binding off there will be one stitch left over that must be counted in the total stitches for the row.

OVERCAST STITCH

Using shawl yarn and holding the pieces to be joined with wrong sides together, take evenly spaced diagonal stitches over the edges of the knitted pieces. If attaching "live" stitches in this manner, make sure the yarn goes through each stitch. Be careful to catch only the edges. Do not pull too tightly or you'll constrict the edge.

PICKING UP STITCHES BY KNITTING

This technique is used to pick up stitches for adding a border to a knitted shawl. Holding the shawl with the right side facing you, insert a needle through an edge stitch from front to back. Wrap the yarn around the needle as if to knit and pull the yarn through, forming a stitch on the needle. Repeat this procedure until the required number of stitches are on the needle.

WASHING, BLOCKING, AND STORING SHAWLS

Having spent the time to knit a beautiful shawl, you should certainly take the time to wash and block it properly. Washing and blocking a shawl are not difficult and the following procedures give the finishing touch to your skillful handwork.

Washing

Always test-wash a swatch of your yarn before washing your shawl. Ideally, you'll have done this before knitting the shawl.

Fill a large sink with warm water, about body temperature. Very cold or very hot water will "shock" fibers, so avoid these extremes. Add one or two teaspoons of your favorite mild soap to the water and mix thoroughly. Place the shawl in the sink, gently push it down into the water, and squeeze to get it thoroughly wet. Let the shawl soak for about ten minutes, then squeeze the soapy water through it a few more times. Let the water drain from the sink and push the shawl against the sides of the sink to remove most of the water. Refill the sink with water that's the same temperature as that used for the wash. Gently knead the shawl, rinsing out the soap. Drain the sink again and repeat this procedure, removing any remaining soap. If a dye is bleeding excessively, simply continue rinsing until the rinse water runs clear. You may add a teaspoon of vinegar to the last rinse to set the dye. To soften wool, use a fabric softener or your hair conditioner in the final rinse. After the final rinse, push the shawl against the sides of the sink to remove most of the water. Do not wring.

To remove more water, roll the shawl in a large towel and squeeze, never twist, allowing the towel to absorb the moisture. Or you may put the shawl in a washing machine and run it through a spin cycle. Be sure to select a slow spin cycle. To protect delicate yarns, put the shawl inside a pillowcase before spinning. Allow the machine to spin for two or three minutes, then remove the shawl.

Blocking

After washing your shawl, lay it out on a blocking board or on a large sheet on the floor. Starting in the center, gently spread the shawl out and pin it into shape with rustproof straight pins or blocking wires. Use a tape measure to check the finished measurements. Let the shawl dry completely.

Storing

Always be sure your shawl is clean before storing it. Soil and body oil attract moths and silverfish, which will damage your garment. Avoid storing your shawl in plastic. Plastic prevents the fibers from "breathing" and that can cause premature aging of yarn and yellowing. Cotton pillowcases or sheets provide the best protection, and they can be washed when they become dusty. Lavender or cedar will deter insects.

Symbols and Abbreviations

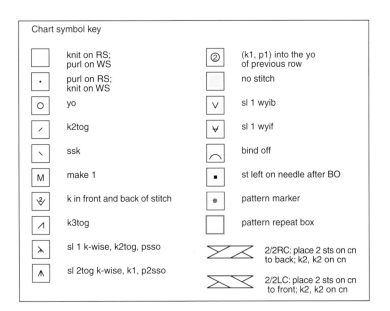

Chart symbol key

☐	knit on RS; purl on WS	②	(k1, p1) into the yo of previous row
·	purl on RS; knit on WS	☐	no stitch
O	yo	V	sl 1 wyib
╱	k2tog	¥	sl 1 wyif
╲	ssk	⌒	bind off
M	make 1	▪	st left on needle after BO
⅋	k in front and back of stitch	•	pattern marker
⟋	k3tog	☐	pattern repeat box
⅄	sl 1 k-wise, k2tog, psso	⧓	2/2RC: place 2 sts on cn to back; k2, k2 on cn
⋀	sl 2tog k-wise, k1, p2sso	⧓	2/2LC: place 2 sts on cn to front; k2, k2 on cn

ABBREVIATIONS

BO	bind off	rep	repeat
CO	cast on	RS	right side
dpn(s)	double pointed needle(s)	sl	slip
k	knit	ssk	slip 2 stitches individually to right needle kwise, slip left needle through front of stitches, and k2tog through back loops
kfb	knit in front and back of stitch		
k2tog	knit 2 stitches together		
kwise	knitwise	st(s)	stitch(es)
m1	make one increase by adding backward loop (see page 13)	St st	stockinette stitch
		wyib	with yarn in back
p	purl	wyif	with yarn in front
psso	pass slipped stitch over	WS	wrong side
p2sso	pass 2 slipped stitches over	yo	yarn over
pwise	purlwise		

Two

The Faroe Islands

Ancient Norwegian sailors passing the foggy cliffs of certain islands in the north Atlantic took the strange creatures flying in and out of the fog to be fairies. In that time fairies were believed to be a powerful race, one to be avoided if at all possible. The sailors named these islands Faroese, old Norwegian for Fairyland, to warn others of the cliffs' inhabitants.

Shawls are as much embedded in the culture and traditions of these islands as the tale of their naming. Faroese natives claim to have invented shawls, and they remain a beautiful part of everyday garb, worn today by young and old, over suits, dresses, and jeans. The Faroese shawl is easy to wear because it hugs your shoulders and won't slide off. It can be worn tied behind the back, pinned with a clasp, or simply draped over the shoulders. Some Faroese shawls are lined for warmth; some shawls are fringed.

The Faroese shawl's shaping is unique. You cast on stitches for the outer edge of the shawl, then work regular decreases every other row to form a triangle with a center back gusset. The effect is of two triangular sections with knitted-on borders joined by a center panel.

These patterns call for a very loose cast-on that prevents the bottom edges from curling under after blocking. Any cast-on method will do as long as it is relaxed and non-binding. Casting on with two needles held together usually produces a very flexible edge. The lace pattern is presented in both written and charted form.

Traditional Faroese shawls are extremely lightweight yet very warm, especially when lined, and any fingering or light sportweight yarn is suitable. They are knitted in a yarn most like laceweight Icelandic or Shetland jumper-weight yarn. Wool, silk, and alpaca also work beautifully, and handspun yarns are very authentic for a Faroese shawl.

To knit the shawls, cast on at the bottom edge and divide into sections with markers. The sections consist of borders, main sections, and the center gusset. The borders and gusset maintain a constant number of stitches except when decreased by the shaping rows. The main sections decrease every other row until only two stitches remain in each main section.

It is important to keep an accurate stitch count, especially when working lace patterns. Stop and count your stitches regularly. Using markers every couple of repeats in the bottom border lace pattern helps to keep the pattern on track.

The shawls are worked in lace-patterned garter stitch. When counting rows, remember that one garter-stitch ridge equals two rows.

The Litla Dimun Shawl employs a traditional shape with Icelandic laceweight wool. The optional lining is knitted separately and the two pieces are sewn together around the outer edges. As is traditional, the lace pattern is presented only in charted form, not written.

The Stóra Dimun Shawl is larger and uses a sportweight silk and wool blend.

Litla Dimun Shawl

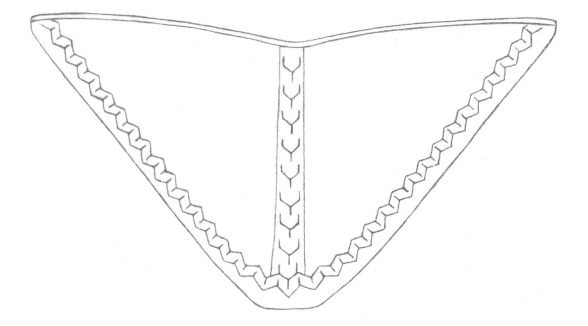

Litla Dimun Shawl

Finished Size About 84" (213 cm) wide at top edge and 29" (73.5 cm) deep at base of gusset.

Yarn Icelandic laceweight wool (100% wool; 1,200 yd [1,097 m]: main color; optional lining color, 1,400 yd [1,280 m].

Needle Size 6 (4 mm): 24" (60-cm) circular. Adjust needle size if necessary to obtain the correct gauge.

Notions Stitch markers; tapestry needle; stitch holders.

Gauge 16 sts and 24 rows = 4" (10 cm) in St st.

Note Only right-side (odd-numbered) rows are charted. Wrong-side (even-numbered) rows are knitted. Slip markers on all rows.

The first marker is a distinguishing color to indicate the beginning of decrease and pattern rows.

All markers remain on needle throughout shawl except when the gusset markers are removed while you're knitting the lace border pattern.

Shawl

Using the cable cast-on (see page 11) or any very flexible method, cast on 421 sts.

Row 1: K8 border sts, place marker (use a unique color here), k190, place marker, k25 (gusset sts), place marker, k190, place marker, knit remaining 8 border sts.

Rows 2, 3, and 4: Knit.

Begin decrease pattern

Row 5: K8, ssk, knit to 2 sts before next marker, k2tog, k25 (gusset sts), ssk, knit to 2 sts before last marker, k2tog, k8.

Row 6 and all even-numbered rows: Knit.

Repeat rows 5 and 6 for a total of 12 ridges (1 garter ridge equals 2 rows) or 24 rows from cast-on edge—381 sts: 8 sts for each border, 170 sts for each main section, and 25 sts for the gusset.

Begin lace border pattern

Note: Decreases are not worked on each side of the gusset throughout the lace border. Remove the markers at the gusset so that they do not interfere with the lace pattern.

Row 25 and all odd-numbered rows through 51: Knit to first marker, follow lace chart to last marker, knit to end.

Row 26 and all even-numbered rows through 50: Knit. You now have 156 sts in each main section.

Replace gusset markers

Row 52: Knit 164 sts, place marker, k25, place marker, k164.

Lace border pattern is complete in main sections at row 52. The lace pattern continues up the back gusset.

Resume gusset decreases

Row 53 and all odd-numbered rows through 59: K8, ssk, knit to 2 sts before gusset marker, k2tog; **work gusset**: follow gusset chart; k2tog; **continue row**: knit to 2 sts before next marker, k2tog, knit to end.

Row 54 and all even-numbered rows through 60: Knit. Stop and read ahead through "shape shoulders."

Work border decreases

Beginning at row 61, work a border decrease every 30 rows. Decrease 1 st by k2tog in each border section before and after the border markers. Repeat these decreases

on rows 91, 121, 151, and 181 until only 3 sts remain in each border.

Row 62: Knit

Row 63: Knit to marker, ssk, knit to 2 sts before next marker, k2tog, work lace pattern over 25 sts, ssk, knit to 2 sts before last marker, k2tog, knit to end.

Row 64: Knit.

Rows 65–70: Repeat rows 63 and 64.

Gusset and shoulder shaping decreases

Now in addition to the regular decreases at the beginning and end of the rows, at each side of the gusset, and in the borders, also work decreases within the gusset and toward the top of the shawl for shoulder shaping.

As shown on chart, beginning on row 71, decrease 2 sts inside gusset. Repeat these decreases on rows 91, 111, 131, 151, and 171—13 sts remain in gusset.

At the same time,

Shape shoulders

Rows 151 and 171: Shape shoulders by decreasing 8 sts evenly spaced in each main section. Decrease by k2tog.

Finishing

Continue to repeat rows 63 and 64 until you have decreased all but 2 sts out of main sections *and at the same time* continue the gusset chart until complete, then work the gusset plain to end of shawl.

When only 2 sts remain in each of the main sections, work the last decrease row by k3tog (the last 2 sts of each main section together with a gusset st). Knit one more plain row. Put all sts except one border (3 sts) on a holder.

Work back and forth on the 3 remaining border sts across the top of the gusset as a border (see knitted-on borders on page 15), knitting 1 st of the border together with 1 st of the gusset (from the holder) on every other row. When all the gusset sts are knitted up, use tapestry needle and Kitchner stitch to graft the 3 border sts together with the 3 border sts on the holder (see page 14). Use tapestry needle to weave in ends. Block.

Optional Lining

Using an invisible cast on (see pages 11–12), cast on 441 sts. Because the lining is worked in plain garter stitch, you need more stitches to compensate for the openness of the lace. Place markers as follows:

Row 1: K8 border sts, place marker (use a unique color here), k200, place marker, k25 (gusset sts), place marker, k200, place marker, knit remaining 8 border sts.

Work as for shawl but without lace pattern. Eliminate the decreases on each side of the gusset on rows 25–52 to make lining same length as shawl. To attach lining to shawl, loosely baste the lining to the shawl then steam both pieces until they match.

Finishing

Using a loose overcast stitch, sew the live cast-on lining sts and the selvedge edges to the shawl edges. Block.

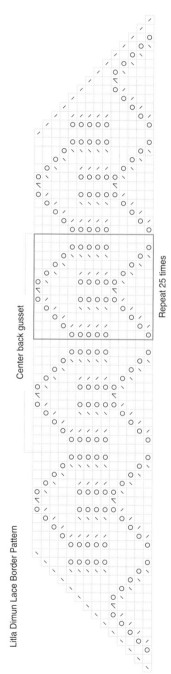

Center back gusset

Litla Dimun Lace Border Pattern

Repeat 25 times

Row 26 and all even-numbered rows: knit

Litla Dimun Lace Gusset Pattern

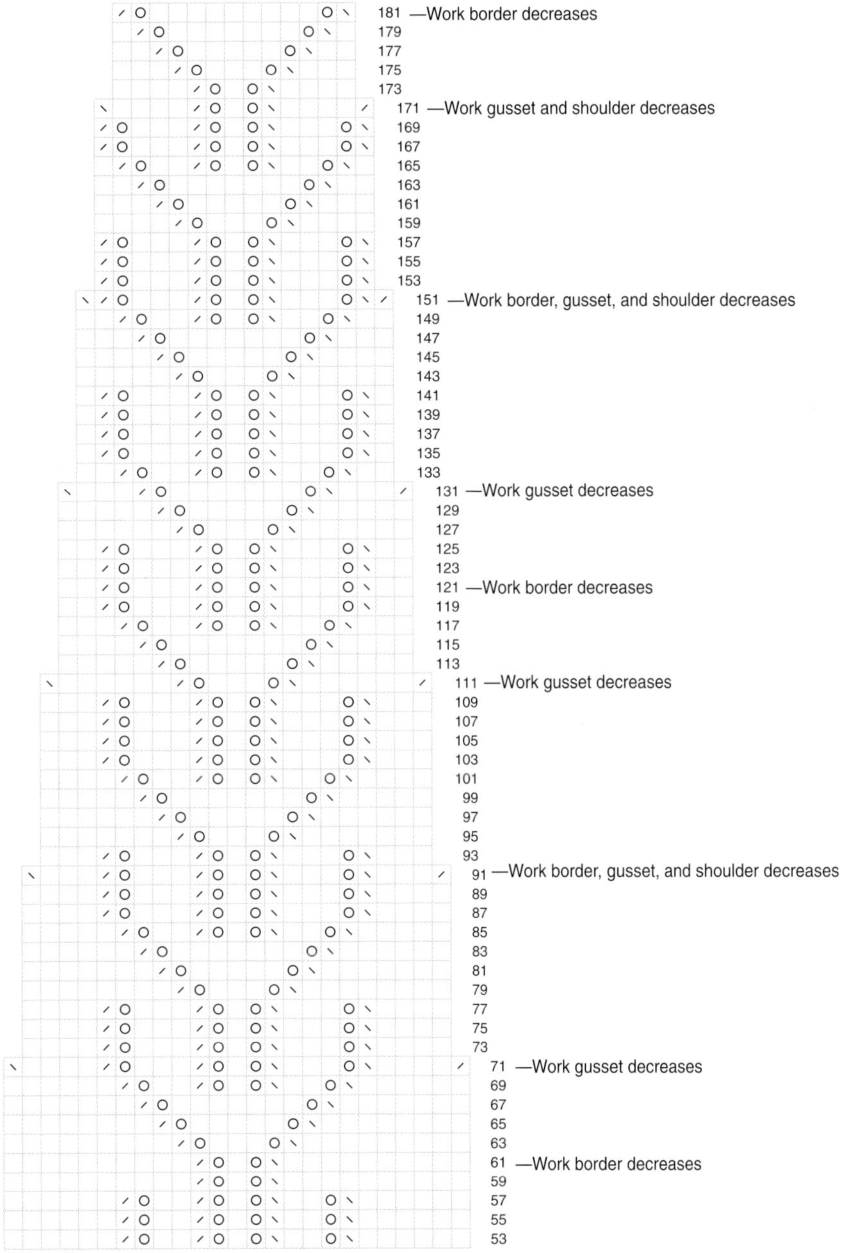

181 —Work border decreases
179
177
175
173
171 —Work gusset and shoulder decreases
169
167
165
163
161
159
157
155
153
151 —Work border, gusset, and shoulder decreases
149
147
145
143
141
139
137
135
133
131 —Work gusset decreases
129
127
125
123
121 —Work border decreases
119
117
115
113
111 —Work gusset decreases
109
107
105
103
101
99
97
95
93
91 —Work border, gusset, and shoulder decreases
89
87
85
83
81
79
77
75
73
71 —Work gusset decreases
69
67
65
63
61 —Work border decreases
59
57
55
53

Row 54 and all even-numbered rows: knit.

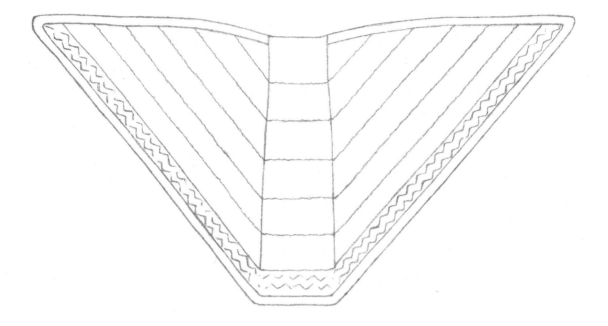

Stóra Dimun Shawl

Finished Size About 86" (218 cm) wide at top edge and 44" (112 cm) deep at base of gusset.

Yarn Blackberry Ridge Woolen Mill Silk Blends, sportweight (75% wool and 25% silk; 375 yd [343 m]/4 oz): red trillium, 3 skeins.

Needle Size 8 (5 mm): 24" (60-cm) circular. Adjust needle size if necessary to obtain the correct gauge.

Notions Stitch markers; tapestry needle; stitch holders.

Gauge 16 sts and 24 rows = 4" (10 cm) in garter stitch.

Note Only right-side (odd-numbered) rows are charted. Wrong-side (even-numbered) rows are knitted. Slip markers on all rows.

The first marker is a distinguishing color to indicate the beginning of decrease and pattern rows.

All markers remain on needle throughout shawl except when the gusset markers are removed while you're knitting the lace border pattern.

Shawl

Cast on 449 sts very loosely (see page 11).

Row 1: K8 border sts, place marker (use a unique color here), k204, place marker, k25 (gusset sts), place marker, k204, place marker, knit remaining 8 border sts.

Rows 2–8: Knit.

Begin decrease rows

Row 9: K8, ssk, knit to 2 sts before next marker, k2tog,

Stóra Dimun Shawl

k25 (gusset sts), ssk, knit to 2 sts before last marker, k2tog, k8.

Row 10: Knit.

Repeat rows 9 and 10 for a total of 11 ridges or 22 rows from cast-on edge—421 sts: 8 sts for each border, 190 sts for each main section, and 25 sts for the gusset.

Begin lace border pattern

Note: Decreases are not worked on each side of the gusset throughout the lace pattern. The lace patterns are presented in both written and charted form. The lace chart covers rows 25 through 63. Only the patterned (odd-numbered) rows are charted; knit all even-numbered rows.

Row 23: K8, ssk, *yo, k2tog, repeat from * to first gusset marker; **work gusset:** *yo, k2tog, repeat from * to 3 sts before second gusset marker, yo, k3tog, yo; **continue row:** *k2tog, yo, repeat from * to 2 sts before last marker, k2tog, k8.

Row 24 and all even-numbered rows: Knit.

Row 25: K8, ssk, knit to 2 sts before last marker, k2tog, k8.

Row 27: K8, ssk, k7, yo, ssk, k7, k2tog, yo, *k1, yo, ssk, k7, k2tog, yo; repeat from * to 9 sts before last marker, k7, k2tog, k8.

Row 29: K8, ssk, k7, yo, ssk, k5, k2tog, yo, k1, *k2, yo, ssk, k5, k2tog, yo, k1; repeat from * to 8 sts before last marker, k6, k2tog, k8.

Row 31: K8, ssk, k5, [yo, ssk] 2 times, k3, [k2tog, yo] 2 times, *k1, [yo, ssk] 2 times, k3, [k2tog, yo] 2 times; repeat from * to 7 sts before last marker, k5, k2tog, k8.

Row 33: K8, ssk, k5, [yo, ssk] 2 times, k1, [k2tog, yo] 2 times, k1, *k2, [yo, ssk] 2 times, k1, [k2tog, yo] 2 times, k1; repeat from * to 6 sts before last marker, k4, k2tog, k8.

Row 35: K8, ssk, k3, [yo, ssk] 2 times, yo, (sl 2, k1,

p2sso), [yo, k2tog] 2 times, yo, *k1, [yo, ssk] 2 times, yo, (sl 2, k1, p2sso), [yo, k2tog] 2 times, yo; repeat from * to 5 sts before last marker, k3, k2tog, k8.

Row 37: K8, ssk, k3, [yo, ssk] 2 times, k1, [k2tog, yo] 2 times, k1, *k2, [yo, ssk] 2 times, k1, [k2tog, yo] 2 times, k1; repeat from * to 4 sts before last marker, k2, k2tog, k8.

Row 39: K8, ssk, *k3, yo, ssk, yo, (sl 2, k1, p2sso), yo, k2tog, yo, k2; repeat from * to 3 sts before last marker, k1, k2tog, k8.

Row 41: K8, ssk, k3, yo, ssk, k1, k2tog, yo, k3, *k4, yo, ssk, k1, k2tog, yo, k3; repeat from * to 2 sts before last marker, k2tog, k8.

Row 43: K8, ssk, k3, yo, (sl 2, k1, p2sso), yo, k4, *k5, yo, (sl 2, k1, p2sso), yo, k4; repeat from * ending last repeat k3, k2tog, k8.

Row 45: K8, ssk, k9, *k1, yo, ssk, k7, k2tog, yo; repeat from * to 12 sts before last marker, k10, k2tog, k8.

Row 47: K8, ssk, k8, *k2, yo, ssk, k5, k2tog, yo, k1; repeat from * to 11 sts before last marker, k9, k2tog, k8.

Row 49: K8, ssk, k7, *k1, [yo, ssk] 2 times, k3, [k2tog, yo] 2 times; repeat from * to 10 sts before last marker, k8, k2tog, k8.

Row 51: K8, ssk, k6, *k2, [yo, ssk] 2 times, k1, [k2tog, yo] 2 times, k1; repeat from * to 9 sts before last marker, k7, k2tog, k8.

Row 53: K8, ssk, k5, *k1, [yo, ssk] 2 times, yo, (sl 2, k1, p2sso), [yo, k2tog] 2 times, yo; repeat from * to 8 sts before last marker, k6, k2tog, k8.

Row 55: K8, ssk, k4, *k2, [yo, ssk] 2 times, k1, [k2tog, yo] 2 times, k1; repeat from * to 7 sts before last marker, k5, k2tog, k8.

Row 57: K8, ssk, k3, *k3, yo, ssk, yo, (sl 2, k1, p2sso), yo, k2tog, yo, k2; repeat from * to 6 sts before last marker, k4, k2tog, k8.

Row 59: K8, ssk, k2, *k4, yo, ssk, k1, k2tog, yo, k3; repeat from * to 5 sts before last marker, k3, k2tog, k8.

Row 61: K8, ssk, k1, *k5, yo, (sl 2, k1, p2sso), yo, k4; repeat from * to 4 sts before last marker, k2, k2tog, k8.

Replace gusset markers

Row 62: Knit 179, place marker, k25, place marker, k179. Lace pattern is complete at row 62.

Resume gusset decreases

Row 63: K8, ssk, knit to 2 sts before last marker, k2tog, k8—169 sts in each main section.

Row 65: K8, ssk, *yo, k2tog; repeat from * to first gusset marker; **work gusset:** *yo, k2tog; repeat from * to 3 sts before second gusset marker, yo, k3tog, yo; **continue row:** *k2tog, yo; repeat from * to 2 sts before last marker, k2tog, k8.

Resume decrease rows

Rows 67–82: Repeat rows 9 and 10 nine times.

Shaping rows and eyelet pattern rows

In addition to the regular row 9 decreases, work extra k2tog decreases as described below on these rows to shape the shawl.

Border and gusset decreases

Rows 83, 103, 123, 143, and 163: Along with regular decreases, decrease 1 st in each border (before first marker and after last marker) and also decrease 1 st inside each edge of gusset.

Eyelet pattern rows

Along with regular decreases, work the eyelet pattern on the following rows. *Note:* On these rows there are sometimes 2 decreases right next to each other.

Rows 85, 105, 125, 145, and 165: Knit to first marker, ssk, *yo, k2tog; repeat from * to 2 sts before gusset marker, k2tog; **work gusset:** *yo, k2tog; repeat from * to last 3 gusset sts, yo, k3tog, yo; **continue row:** ssk, *k2tog, yo; repeat from * to 2 sts before last marker, k2tog, knit to end of row.

Shape shoulders

Rows 155 and 175: Shape shoulders by decreasing 10 extra sts evenly spaced in each main section. Decrease by k2tog.

Finishing

When only 2 sts remain in each of the main sections, work the last decrease row by k3tog (the last 2 sts of each main section together with a gusset st). Put all sts except one border (3 sts) on a holder.

Work back and forth on the 3 remaining border sts across the top of the gusset as a border (see knitted-on borders on page 15), knitting 1 st of the border together with 1 st of the gusset (from the holder) on every other row. When all the gusset sts are knitted up, use tapestry needle and Kitchner stitch to graft the 3 border sts together with the 3 border sts on the holder (see page 14). Use tapestry needle to weave in ends. Block.

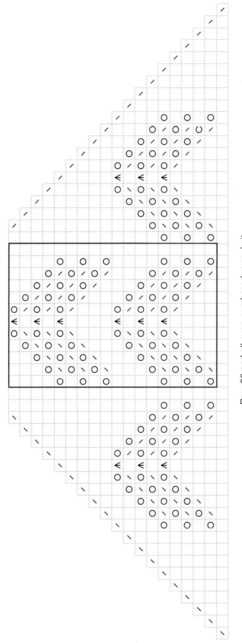

61 59 57 55 53 51 49 47 45 43 41 39 37 35 33 31 29 27 25

Row 26 and all even-numbered rows: knit.

Stóra Dimun Lace Pattern

Three

Ireland

According to Irish folklore, if a master knitter places knitting needles in a newborn baby's hands, the child will acquire a talent for knitting. Female babies were often given knitting needles so that they would have skills with which to help support themselves and their families.

In the late nineteenth century, a conscientious mother discovered that the local master knitter was reluctant to pass on her talents. To convince her, the mother plied the elderly knitter with a home-brewed liquor called *poteen*. By the time the old woman had consented, she was so tipsy that she put the knitting needles in the baby's left hand. Although right-handed in everything else, the baby grew into a left-handed knitter.

Irish Diamond Shawl

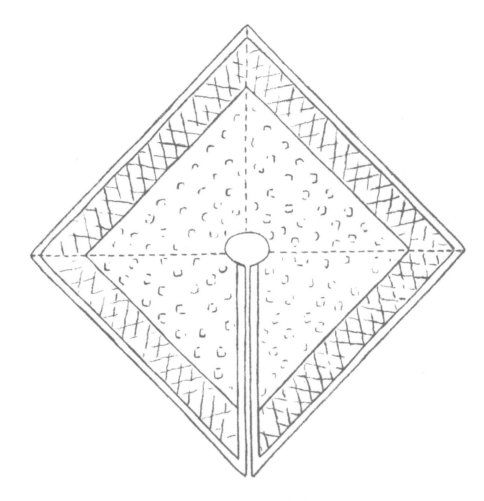

Irish Diamond Shawl

Inspired by a modern woven Irish shawl, this lace-patterned shawl is worked from the neckband down. It is shaped with yarnover increases worked at the center front, center back, and each side "seam." The first six and last six stitches of each row are worked in garter stitch and form the front border (which mimics the neck and lower edge borders). The lace patterns are worked in the large sections and do not interfere with the increases.

Finished Size About 52" (132 cm) square.

Yarn Harrisville Designs Shetland (100% wool; 900 yd [823 m]/8-oz cone): hemlock, 2,200 yd.

Needle Size 7 (4.5 mm): 24" or 32" (60-cm or 80-cm) circular. Adjust needle size if necessary to obtain the correct gauge.

Notions Stitch markers; tapestry needle.

Gauge 16 sts and 24 rows = 4" (10 cm) in St st.

Note Only right-side (odd-numbered) rows are charted. Slip markers on all rows. The markers indicate the orners of the shawl. The two corner stitches between the markers are maintained as knit stitches throughout the shawl. The yarnover increases and the lace patterns are worked in the four large sections on either side of the markers.

Neckband
Cast on 74 sts loosely (see page 11).

Row 1: K6, place marker, [yo, k14, place marker, k2, place marker] 3 times, yo, k14, yo, place marker, k6.

Row 2 and all WS rows: Knit.

Row 3: K6, [yo, k16, yo, k2] 3 times, yo, k16, yo, k6.

Row 5: K6, [yo, k18, yo, k2] 3 times, yo, k18, yo, k6.

Row 7: K6, [yo, k20, yo, k2] 3 times, yo, k20, yo, k6—106 sts. Neckband complete.

Begin lace patterns
The first six stitches and the last six stitches of every row are knitted to form a garter-stitch border. Work the lace patterns in the sections between the corner markers. The sections are increased every other row by making yarnovers on each side of the k2 "seam" stitches. The lace patterns are presented in both written and charted form.

Lace pattern 1
Row 1: K6, [yo, k3, *k3, yo, ssk, k3; repeat from * to 3 sts before next marker, k3, yo, k2 (corner sts)] 4 times, end last repeat k6—114 sts.

Row 2 and all WS rows: K6, purl to last marker, k6.

Row 3: K6, [yo, k4, *k1, k2tog, yo, k1, yo, ssk, k2; repeat from * to 4 sts before marker, k4, yo, k2] 4 times, end last repeat k6—122 sts.

Row 5: K6, [yo, k5, *k2tog, yo, k3, yo, ssk, k1; repeat from * to 5 sts before marker, k5, yo, k2] 4 times, end last repeat k6—130 sts.

Row 7: K6, [yo, k6, *k2, yo, sl 2tog kwise, k1, p2sso, yo,

k3; repeat from * to 6 sts before marker, k6, yo, k2] 4 times, end last repeat k6—138 sts.

Rows 9–112: Repeat Rows 1–8 thirteen more times—134 sts in each large section (15 diamonds across).

Row 113: K6, [*yo, k134, yo, k2] 4 times, end last repeat k6—562 sts; 136 sts in each large section.

Eyelet 1
Row 115: K6, [yo, k1, *(yo, k2tog); repeat from * to 1 st before next marker, k1, yo, k2] 4 times, end last repeat k6—138 sts in each large section.

Row 117: K6, [yo, knit to next marker, yo, k2] 4 times, end last repeat k6—140 sts in each large section.

Lace pattern 2
Row 119: K6, [yo, k4, *yo, ssk, k7, k2tog, yo, k1; repeat from * to 4 sts before marker, k4, yo, k2] 4 times, end last repeat k6—142 sts in each large section.

Row 121: K6, [yo, k5, *k1, yo, ssk, k5, k2tog, yo, k2; repeat from * to 5 sts before marker, k5, yo, k2] 4 times, end last repeat k6—144 sts in each large section.

Row 123: K6, [yo, k6, *(yo, ssk) 2 times, k3, (k2tog, yo) 2 times, k1; repeat from * to 6 sts before marker, k6, yo, k2] 4 times, end last repeat k6—146 sts in each large section.

Row 125: K6, [yo, k7, *k1, (yo, ssk) 2 times, k1, (k2tog, yo) 2 times, k2; repeat from * to 7 sts before marker, k7, yo, k2] 4 times, end last repeat k6—148 sts in each large section.

Row 127: K6, [yo, k8, *(yo, ssk) 2 times, yo, sl 1, k2tog, p2sso, yo, (k2tog, yo) 2 times, k1; repeat from * to 8 sts before marker, k8, yo, k2] 4 times, end last repeat k6—150 sts in each large section.

Row 129: K6, [yo, k9, *k3, k2tog, yo, k1, yo, ssk, k4; repeat from * to 9 sts before marker, k9, yo, k2] 4 times, end last repeat k6—152 sts in each large section.

Row 131: K6, [yo, k10, *k2, k2tog, yo, k3, yo, ssk, k3;

repeat from * to 10 sts before marker, k10, yo, k2] 4 times, end last repeat k6—154 sts in each large section.

Row 133: K6, [yo, k11, *k1, (k2tog, yo) 2 times, k1, (yo, ssk) 2 times, k2; repeat from * to 11 sts before marker, k11, yo, k2] 4 times, end last repeat k6—156 sts in each large section.

Row 135: K6, [yo, k12, *(k2tog, yo) 2 times, k3, (yo, ssk) 2 times, k1; repeat from * to 12 sts before marker, k12, yo, k2] 4 times, end last repeat k6—158 sts in each large section.

Row 137: K6, [yo, k12, k2tog, *(yo, k2tog) 2 times, yo, k1, yo, (ssk, yo) 2 times, sl 1, k2tog, psso; repeat from * to 24 sts before marker, (yo, k2tog) 2 times, yo, k1, (yo, ssk) 3 times, k13, yo, k2] 4 times, end last repeat k6—160 sts in each large section.

Row 139: K6, [yo, k2, *yo, ssk, k7, k2tog, yo, k1; repeat from * to 2 sts before marker, k2, yo, k2] 4 times, end last repeat k6—162 sts in each large section.

Row 141: K6, [yo, k3, *k1, yo, ssk, k5, k2tog, yo, k2; repeat from * to 3 sts before marker, k3, yo, k2] 4 times, end last repeat k6—164 sts in each large section.

Row 143: K6, [yo, k4, *(yo, ssk) 2 times, k3, (k2tog, yo) 2 times, k1; repeat from * to 4 sts before marker, k4, yo, k2] 4 times, end last repeat k6—166 sts in each large section.

Row 145: K6, [yo, k5, *k1, (yo, ssk) 2 times, k1, (k2tog, yo) 2 times, k2; repeat from * to 5 sts before marker, k5, yo, k2] 4 times, end last repeat k6—168 sts in each large section.

Row 147: K6, [yo, k6, *(yo, ssk) 2 times, yo, sl 1, k2tog, p2sso, yo, (k2tog, yo) 2 times, k1; repeat from * to 6 sts before marker, k6, yo, k2] 4 times, end last repeat k6—170 sts in each large section.

Row 149: K6, [yo, k7, *k3, k2tog, yo, k1, yo, ssk, k4; repeat from * to 7 sts before marker, k7, yo, k2] 4 times, end last repeat k6—172 sts each large section.

Row 151: K6, [yo, k8, *k2, k2tog, yo, k3, yo, ssk, k3; repeat from * to 8 sts before marker, k8, yo, k2] 4 times, end last repeat k6—174 sts each large section.

Row 153: K6, [yo, k9, *k1, (k2tog, yo) 2 times, k1, (yo, ssk) 2 times, k2; repeat from * to 9 sts before marker, k9, yo, k2] 4 times, end last repeat k6—176 sts each large section.

Row 155: K6, [yo, k10, *(k2tog, yo) 2 times, k3, (yo, ssk) 2 times, k1; repeat from * to 10 sts before marker, k10, yo, k2] 4 times, end last repeat k6—178 sts each large section.

Row 157: K6, [yo, k10, k2tog, *(yo, k2tog) 2 times, yo, k1, yo, (ssk, yo) 2 times, sl 1, k2tog, psso; repeat from * to 22 sts before marker, (yo, k2tog) 2 times, yo, k1, (yo, ssk) 3 times, k11, yo, k2] 4 times, end last repeat k6—180 sts in each large section.

Row 159: K6, [yo, knit to next marker, yo, k2] 4 times, end last repeat k6—182 sts in each large section.

Eyelet 2

Row 161: K6, [yo, k1, *yo, k2tog; repeat from * to 1 st before marker, k1, yo, k2] 4 times, end last repeat k6—184 sts in each large section.

Row 163: K6, [yo, knit to next marker, yo, k2] 4 times, end last repeat k6—186 sts in each large section.

Garter stitch border

Knit 12 rows. Bind off very loosely. Use tapestry needle to weave in ends. Block.

Irish Diamond Lace Pattern

Lace Diamond Pattern 2 continued

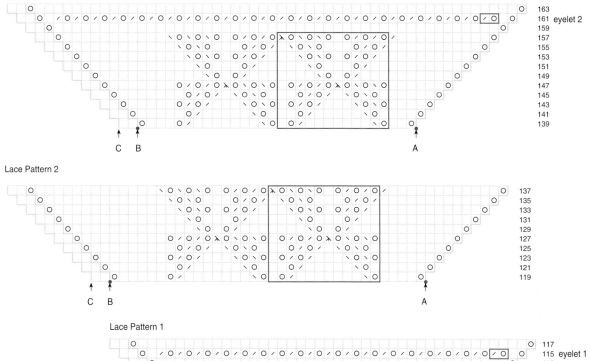

163
161 eyelet 2
159
157
155
153
151
149
147
145
143
141
139

C B   A

Lace Pattern 2

137
135
133
131
129
127
125
123
121
119

C B   A

Lace Pattern 1

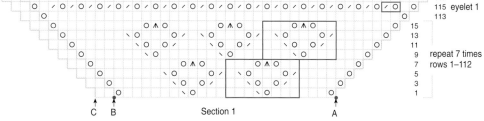

117
115 eyelet 1
113
15
13
11
9   repeat 7 times
7   rows 1–112
5
3
1

C B   Section 1   A

Shawl is composed of 4 sections and 6-stitch garter borders. Section 1 is shown. Directions below complete all 4 sections.

All odd-numbered rows: k6, repeat from A to C of Lace Pattern 1 chart 3 times, then work from A to B once, end k6.

All even-numbered rows (not shown on chart): k6, purl to last marker, k6.

Continue with Lace Pattern 1 chart until there are 15 diamonds (highlighted box) across each section. Work through row 118.

Lace Pattern 2 chart: k6, repeat from A to C of Lace Pattern 2 chart 3 times, then work from A to B once, end k6.

Lace Pattern 2 chart continued: k6, repeat from A to C of Lace Pattern 2 chart continued 3 times, then work from A to B once, end k6.

Knit 12 rows.

Kilkenny Cable Shawl

Kilkenny Cable Shawl

On the Aran Islands, one traditional mode of dress is a red skirt with a dark shawl. This shawl uses an Aran-weight yarn spun in County Kilkenny. This is a real Irish yarn with a very crisp hand. The Kilkenny Cable Shawl is rectangular and has a cable and lace pattern and a knitted-on seed stitch border.

Finished Size About 72" (183 cm) long and 31" (79 cm) wide.

Yarn Black Water Abbey Yarn (100% wool, 220 yd [201 m]/4 oz): old navy, 7 skeins.

Needles Size 7 (4.5 mm): 32" (80-cm) circular. Size 5 (3.75 mm): 32" (80-cm) circular. Adjust needle size if necessary to obtain the correct gauge.

Notions Stitch markers; tapestry needle.

Gauge 16 sts and 22 rows = 4" (10 cm) in St st.

Note Slip markers on all rows.

Abbreviations

2/2LC: Put 2 sts on cable needle and hold in front, k2, then k2 from the cable needle.

2/2RC: Put 2 sts on cable and hold in back, k2, then k2 from the cable needle.

Stitches

Seed stitch (on an even # of sts)

Row 1: *K1, p1; repeat from * to end.

Row 2: *P1, k1; repeat from * to end.
  Repeat Rows 1 and 2 for pattern.

Pattern stitch (multiple of 14 sts plus 6)

Row 1 (RS): *P2, k2tog, yo, p2, 2/2LC, 2/2RC; repeat from * to 6 sts before last marker, end p2, k2tog, yo, p2.

Rows 2 and 4: *K2, p2, k2, p8; repeat from * to 6 sts before last marker, end k2, p2, k2.

Row 3: *P2, yo, ssk, p2, k8; repeat from * to 6 sts before last marker, end p2, yo, ssk, p2.

Repeat Rows 1–4 for pattern.

Shawl

Using smaller needle, cast on 308 sts loosely (see page 11). Work in seed stitch for 12 rows. On next row work seed stitch, placing markers as follows: Work 8 sts, place marker, work to last 8 sts, place marker, work 8 sts. On the next row work in seed stitch increasing as follows:

Work 18 sts, kfb, *work 13 sts, kfb; repeat from * 20 more times, work 17 sts—330 sts. Change to larger needle.

Maintain the seed stitch borders on the first and last 8 sts of each row. The cable and lace pattern is presented in both written and charted form and is worked on the 314 sts between the markers.

Work in pattern until shawl measures about 28" (71 cm) from cast-on edge, ending with row 1. Change to smaller needle and work in seed stitch, dec in the next row as follows: Work 17 sts, k2tog, *work 12 sts, k2tog; repeat from * 20 more times, work 17 sts—308 sts. Work 13 rows of seed stitch. Bind off loosely.

Finishing

Use tapestry needle to weave in ends. Block.

Kilkenny Cable and Lace Pattern

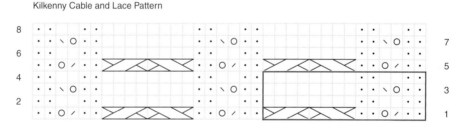

Maintain seed stitch borders on the first and last 8 sts of each row.

𝔄ran 𝔓ocket 𝔖hawl

Aran Pocket Shawl

Women on the Aran Islands often wear woven plaid shawls from Scotland. The basket weave pattern and the pockets on this shawl are based on a modern Scottish woven plaid shawl.

Finished Size About 87" (221 cm) long and 22" (56 cm) wide.

Yarn Black Water Abbey Yarn (100% wool; 220 yd [201 m]/4 oz): bluestack, 7 skeins.

Needles Size 8 (5 mm): 24" (60-cm) circular. Size 7 (4.5 mm): 24" (60-cm) circular. Adjust needle size if necessary to obtain the correct gauge.

Notions Stitch markers; tapestry needle.

Gauge 16 sts and 24 rows = 4" (10 cm) in St st.

Note: Slip markers on all rows.

Stitches

Seed stitch (on an even # of sts)

Row 1: *K1, p1; repeat from * to end.

Row 2: *P1, k1; repeat from * to end.

Repeat rows 1 and 2 for pattern.

Pattern stitch (multiple of 14 sts plus 2)

Rows 1, 3, and 5: K2, *(p1, k1) 2 times, p1, k2; repeat from *.

Rows 2, 4, and 6: *P3, (k1, p1) 2 times; repeat from *, end last repeat p3.

Row 7: K2, *p12, k2; repeat from *.

Row 8: Knit the knits and purl the purls as they appear.

Row 9: Knit.

Rows 10, 12, and 14: *P2, (k1, p1) 2 times, k1; repeat from *, end p2.

Rows 11, 13, and 15: K2, *(k1, p1) 2 times, k3; repeat from *.

Row 16: *K7, p2, k5; repeat from * end last repeat k7.

Row 17: Knit the knits and purl the purls as they appear.

Row 18: Purl.

Repeat rows 1–18 for pattern.

Shawl

With smaller needle, cast on 86 sts loosely (see page 11). Work 7 rows seed stitch. Maintain the seed stitch borders on the first and last 7 sts of each row. The pattern stitch, which may be worked from the written instructions or the chart, is worked on the 72 sts between the markers.

Repeat 18-row pattern 27 times, then work rows 1–16 once more. Change to smaller needle and work 7 rows seed stitch. Bind off loosely in pattern.

Pockets (make two)

With larger needle, cast on 44 sts and work 18-row pattern 2 times. Change to smaller needle and work 8 rows seed stitch for top border. Bind off in purl.

Finishing

Use tapestry needle to weave in ends. Block.

Try shawl on to determine the pocket placement as shown on illustration and mark highest corner. To achieve the correct angle, the high corner of the pocket bottom should be about 2½" (6.5 cm) above the low corner. Using tapestry needle, sew pockets to right side of shawl.

Aran Pocket Shawl Pattern

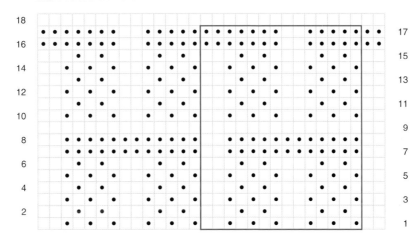

Maintain seed stitch borders on the first and last 7 sts of each row.

Four

Japan

𝔎𝔦𝔪𝔬𝔫𝔬 𝔖𝔥𝔞𝔴𝔩

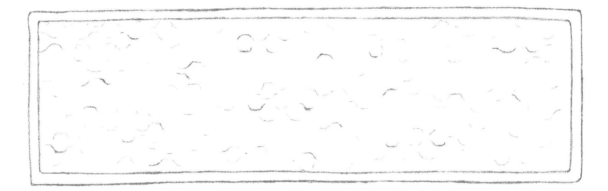

***Chado*, the Japanese** tea ceremony, has been developed over centuries to create an atmosphere of peace and harmony, to engage participants in the beauty of the moment.

Traditional dress for the tea ceremony is the formal kimono, and kimono shawls are worn in spring and autumn as an outer garment. The shawl is removed once one has enjoyed the tea garden and entered the teahouse, and it is left in a special room. Delicate rectangular lace shawls, knitted or woven from spun silk, are a favorite. The shawl presented here has knitted-on garter-stitch borders.

Knitting needles click;

a cup of tea scents the air.

The new shawl begins!

Kimono Shawl

Finished Size About 72" (183 cm) long and 22" (56 cm) wide.

Yarn Henry's Attic Cascade (100% spun silk; 1,000 yd [915 m]/8-oz hank): natural, 2 hanks.

Needle Size 5 (3.75 mm): 24" (60-cm) circular. Adjust needle size if necessary to obtain the correct gauge.

Notions Stitch markers; tapestry needle.

Gauge 21 sts and 30 rows = 4" (10 cm) in blocked pattern st; 20 sts and 30 rows = 4" in St st.

Note Only right-side (odd-numbered) rows are charted. Wrong-side (even-numbered) rows are purled. Slip markers on all rows.

Lace pattern (multiple of 10 sts plus 1)
Row 1: *K3, k2tog, yo, k1, yo, ssk, k2; repeat from * end last repeat k3.

Row 2 and all WS rows: Purl.

Row 3: *K2, k2tog, yo, k3, yo, ssk, k1; repeat from * end last repeat k2.

Row 5: *K1, k2tog, yo, k5, yo, ssk; repeat from * end k1.

Rows 7, 9, and 11: *K1, ssk, k2, yo, k1, yo, k2, k2tog; rep from * end k1.

Row 13: *K1, yo, ssk, k5, k2tog, yo; repeat from * end k1.

Row 15: *K2, yo, ssk, k3, k2tog, yo, k1; repeat from * end last repeat k2.

Row 17: *K3, yo, ssk, k1, k2tog, yo, k2; repeat from * end last repeat k3.

Rows 19, 21, and 23: *K1, yo, k2, k2tog, k1, ssk, k2, yo; repeat from * end k1.

Shawl

Cast on 117 sts loosely (see page 11). Work 20 rows in garter st ending on a WS row *and at the same time* work last row as follows: k8, place marker, k101, place marker, k8. Maintain garter st border on first and last 8 sts of each row. The pattern stitch is presented in both written and charted form and is worked on the 101 sts between the markers. Repeat 24-row pattern 25 times or to desired length. Work 20 rows in garter st. Bind off loosely.

Finishing

Use tapestry needle to weave in ends. Block.

Kimono Shawl Lace Pattern

All odd-numbered rows: k8, repeat stitches in highlighted box, end k8.
All even-numbered rows (not shown on chart): k8, purl to last marker, k8.

Five

The American Heartland

Heartland Shawl

Before the twentieth century, knitters did not always have the benefit of written patterns to work from—and the few patterns that did exist were sketchy. Patterns could be as vague as one from the 1850s that told the knitter to cast on about 320 stitches and knit using a lace pattern that had better be simple. Adding a brightly colored border would "greatly enhance" the shawl. Presented here is one interpretation of those instructions.

Heartland Shawl

The Heartland Shawl is a basic large rectangle in a medium-weight, neutral color yarn with a brightly colored edging. The lace patterns are simple but effective. This shawl includes a picot edge.

Finished Size About 90" (229 cm) long and 35" (89 cm) wide.

Yarn Nature Spun Sport (100% wool; 184 yd [168 m]/ 1¾ oz): grey heather, 10 skeins for shawl; sapphire, 2 skeins for border, waste yarn.

Needles Shawl: Size 5 (3.75 mm): 32" (80-cm) circular. Border: Three size 4 (3.5 mm) 24" (60-cm) circular. Adjust needle size if necessary to obtain the correct gauge.

Notions Stitch markers; tapestry needle; waste yarn.

Gauge 18 sts and 26 rows = 4" (10 cm) in St st.

Note Only right-side (odd-numbered) rows are charted. Work wrong-side (even-numbered) rows as follows: Sl 1, purl to end. Slip markers on all rows.

Pattern stitch (multiple of 6 sts plus 3)

Note: Slip the first stitch of every row purlwise with yarn in front.

Row 1: Sl 1, k3, *yo, ssk, k4; repeat from * end last repeat k3.

Row 2 and all even-numbered rows: Sl 1, purl to end.

Row 3: Sl 1, k1, k2tog, yo, *k1, yo, ssk, k1, k2tog, yo; repeat from * end k1, yo, ssk, k2.

Row 5: Sl 1, k2tog, yo, k1, *k2, yo, (sl 1, k2tog, psso), yo, k1; repeat from *, end k2, yo, ssk, k1.

Rows 7 and 9: Sl 1, k1, yo, ssk, *k1, k2tog, yo, k1, yo, ssk; repeat from * end k1, k2tog, yo, k2.

Repeat rows 1-10 for pattern.

Shawl

Cast on 321 sts using an invisible method (see pages 11–12). Repeat 10-row pattern 25 times, leave sts on needle.

Border

The border is picked up and knitted in the round in circular garter stitch (see Picking up Stitches by Knitting on page 15). The corners are mitered by increasing on each side of the corner stitches on every other round. While it may seem that there are an enormous number of stitches on the needle, the border is only 11 rounds deep so you'll complete it in a jiffy. To make handling so many stitches easier, use two border needles to hold the stitches (put stoppers or rubber bands on the ends to keep the stitches from slipping off between rounds) and knit with the third. The picot bind-off gives a special finish.

With border yarn and smaller needle, knit the 321 sts, marking the first and last sts for the corners; with the same needle, pick up 187 sts along the first short side of the shawl as follows: Pick up in 1 slipped st, *make 1, pick up in next 2 slipped sts; repeat from *, end make 1, pick up in 1 slipped st. Remove waste yarn and mark the first and last sts for the corners. With second border needle, knit across invisibly cast-on sts and, with the same needle, pick up 187 sts along the second short side of the shawl as for first short side—1016 sts on two needles. Join, placing a uniquely-colored marker to indicate beginning of round, and work circular garter stitch as follows:

Rnd 1: Purl.

Rnd 2: K1 (corner stitch), m1, *knit to next marked st, m1, k1 (corner st), m1; repeat from * ending last repeat knit to next marked st, m1.

Repeat rnds 1 and 2 four more times, then work rnd 1 once more.

Picot bind-off

K1, *[yo, slip previous st over yo] 3 times, bind off next 2 sts; repeat from *.

Finishing

Use tapestry needle to weave in ends. Block.

Heartland Shawl Lace Pattern

Row 2 and all even-numbered rows: Sl 1 wyif, purl to end.

Prairie Shawls

American pioneer settlers were by necessity extremely practical people, and women often wore shawls in place of more restrictive and less versatile coats. For everyday work and travel, women needed heavy shawls in a "practical color." These Prairie Shawls fill the bill. The yarn used resembles homespun and the pattern and shapings are simple.

The inspiration for these shawls was one shawl found in a dusty corner of an antique shop in the Minnesota countryside. The little shawl presented itself as just a flash of pale pink knitted fabric with a two-dollar price tag. It was a treasure indeed, and you could tell by the numerous mendings that it had been a well-loved garment. The shawl is simplicity itself and very much a part of the tradition of everyday folk shawls around the world. The shaping is intriguing and the shawl has proved to be a joy to knit. Prairie Shawls provide a wonderful canvas for all kinds of lace possibilities.

Simple Garter Stitch Prairie Shawl

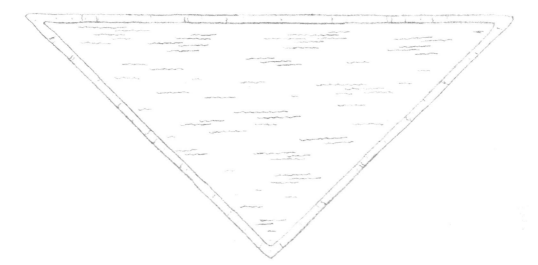

Simple Garter Stitch Prairie Shawl

Finished Size About 77" (196 cm) wide at top edge and 37" (94 cm) deep at point.

Yarn Wool Pak Yarn N.Z. 8 ply (100% wool; 525 yds [480 m]/250 g): navy, 3 skeins.

Needle Size 8 (5 mm): 24" (60-cm) circular or straight. Adjust needle size if necessary to obtain the correct gauge.

Notions Tapestry needle.

Gauge 16 sts and 28 rows = 4" (10 cm) in garter st.

The shawl is worked from the bottom to the top in garter stitch. Work increases by kfb on rows 1–13 until the border point is formed, then use yarnovers for the remaining increases.

Shawl

Cast on 3 sts.

Row 1: Kfb, k1, kfb—5 sts.
Row 2 and all WS rows: Knit.
Row 3: Kfb, knit to last st, kfb—7 sts.
Rows 5–12: Repeat Rows 3 and 4—15 sts.
Row 13: Kfb, knit to the end—16 sts.
Row 15: K8, yo, k8—17 sts.
Row 17: K8, yo, k1, yo, k8—19 sts.
Row 19: K8, yo, knit to last 8 sts, yo, k8—21 sts.
Row 20: Knit.
Rows 21–274: Repeat rows 19 and 20—275 sts.
Row 275: K8, yo, k1, *yo, k2tog, repeat from * to last 8 sts, yo, k8—277 sts.

Repeat rows 19 and 20 six times—289 sts.

Knit 12 rows garter stitch. Bind off loosely (use a larger needle to bind off if necessary).

Finishing

Use tapestry needle to weave in ends. Block.

Lacy Prairie Shawl

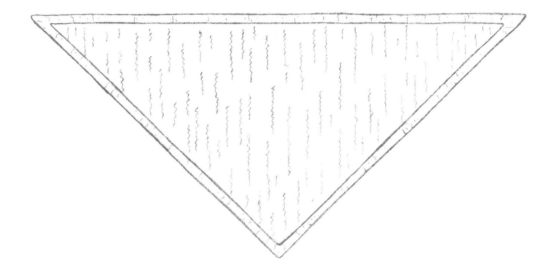

Lacy Prairie Shawl

Finished Size About 77" (196 cm) wide at top edge and 37" (94 cm) deep at point.

Yarn Wool Pak Yarn N.Z. 8 ply; (100% wool; 525 yd [480 m]/250 g): natural, 2 skeins

Needle Size 8 (5 mm): 24" (60-cm) circular. Adjust needle size if necessary to obtain the correct gauge.

Notion Tapestry needle.

Gauge 14 sts and 28 rows = 4" (10 cm) in garter stitch

The shawl is worked from the bottom to the top in a simple garter-stitch lace inside garter-stitch borders. Work increases by kfb on rows 1–19 until the border point is formed, then use yarnovers for the remaining increases. The lace begins on row 33.

Note Only right-side (odd-numbered) rows are charted. Wrong-side (even-numbered) rows are knitted. Slip markers on all rows.

Shawl

Cast on 3 sts.

Row 1: Kfb, k1, kfb—5 sts.

Row 2 and all WS rows: Knit.

Row 3: Kfb, knit to last st, kfb—7 sts.

Rows 5–18: Repeat rows 3 and 4 seven times—21 sts.

Row 19: Kfb, knit to the end of the row—22 sts.

Row 21: K11, yo, k11—23 sts.

Row 23: K11, yo, k1, yo, k11—25 sts.

Row 25: K11, yo, k3, yo, k11—27 sts.

Row 27: K11, yo, k5, yo, k11—29 sts.

Row 29: K11, yo, k7, yo, k11—31 sts.

Row 31: K11, yo, k9, yo, k11—33 sts.

Row 33: K11, yo, k4, yo, (sl 2, k1, p2sso), yo, k4, yo, k11—35 sts.

Row 35: K11, yo, k2, yo, (sl 2, k1, p2sso), yo, k3, yo, (sl 2, k1, p2sso), yo, k2, yo, k11—37 sts.

Row 37: K11, yo, k6, yo, (sl 2, k1, p2sso), yo, k6, yo, k11—39 sts.

Row 39: K11, yo, k4, yo, (sl 2, k1, p2sso), yo, k3, yo,

(sl 2, k1, p2sso), yo, k4, yo, k11—41 sts.

Row 41: K11, yo, k2, *yo, (sl 2, k1, p2sso), yo, k3; repeat from *, end last repeat k2, yo, k11—43 sts.

Row 43: K11, yo, k3, *k3, yo, (sl 2, k1, p2sso), yo; repeat from *, end last repeat k6, yo, k11—45 sts.

Row 45: K11, yo, k4, *yo, (sl 2, k1, p2sso), yo, k3; repeat from *, end last repeat k4, yo, k11—47 sts.

Repeat rows 41–46 thirty-eight more times until there are 275 sts.

Next row: K11, yo, k1, *yo, k2tog; repeat from * to last 11 sts, yo, k11—277 sts.

Top border

Row 1: K11, yo, knit to last 11 sts, yo, k11.

Row 2: Knit.

Repeat rows 1 and 2 five more times—289 sts.

Bind off loosely (use a larger needle to bind off if necessary).

Finishing

Use tapestry needle to weave in ends. Block.

Lacy Prarie shawl

Maintain garter stitch borders on the first and last 11 stitches of all rows.
Row 34 and all even-numbered rows: knit.
Work increases into pattern as indicated by highlighted box.
Repeat rows 41-46 thirty-eight more times.

Six

Iceland

The folklore of Iceland holds that fairy women could travel between Earth and Fairyland on their shawls. They would lay their most beautiful shawls on the ground in a boggy area, then stand in the center. The shawls would sink into the bog and the fairies would be safely (and dryly!) transported to their underground kingdom. To return, they again stood on the shawls and rose through the bog to the human realm.

Icelandic shawls are distinctive in both pattern and materials. Bands of color, usually natural sheep colors, blend gracefully into each other. A stitch pattern that creates a wavy line often adds to the beauty of the neutral shadings. Unspun Icelandic yarn is similar to fine roving that is ready to spin. Before it is knitted, it is weak and easily broken. Once knitted, however, the tension on the stitches gives it an amazing strength. Like any roving, if you pull on it with only a short distance between your hands, it is almost impossible to break; the farther apart you hold your hands, the easier it is to pull apart. Even a cat walking across a stretched-out strand of unspun Icelandic yarn can cause it to break! Broken strands are easily rejoined by fraying the broken ends, laying them across each other, and rubbing the area of the splice briskly between the palms. Like magic the yarn is whole again. The very qualities that make unspun initially tricky to work with are also what make it such a wonderful knitted fiber. Since it is not as dense as spun yarn, it is light as a feather and luxuriously warm at the same time. Try it. You may become a fan!

Feather and Fan Shawl

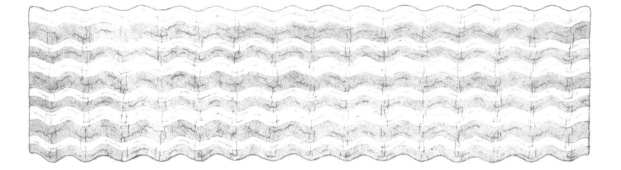

Feather and Fan Shawl

This lace-patterned rectangular shawl uses unspun Icelandic wool in two shades. The shawl is knitted from one long edge to the other, and the pattern bands are horizontal. Color changes are made on right-side rows.

Finished Size About 88" (224 cm) long and 28" (71 cm) wide

Yarn Unspun Icelandic wool (100% wool; 300 yd [274 m]/3½ oz): silver gray, medium gray, 2 wheels each.

Needle Size 8 (5 mm): 32" (80-cm) circular. Adjust needle size if necessary to obtain the correct gauge.

Notions Stitch markers; tapestry needle.

Gauge 16 sts and 24 rows = 4" (10 cm) in St st.

Note All rows are charted. Three repeats of 4-row pattern are shown on chart. Slip markers on all rows.

Stitch pattern (multiple of 18 sts)

Set-Up Row: Knit.

Row 1 (RS): Knit.

Row 2: Purl.

Row 3: *[K2 tog] 3 times, [yo, k1] 6 times, [k2 tog] 3 times; repeat from *.

Row 4: Knit.

Repeat Rows 1–4 for pattern.

Color sequence

Note: Color changes are made on row 1. One repeat equals 4 pattern rows worked once.

Rows 1–16: 4 repeats of silver gray.

Rows 17–32: 4 repeats of medium gray.

Rows 33–40: 2 repeats of silver gray.

Rows 41–48: 2 repeats of medium gray.

Shawl

With silver gray, cast on 390 sts.

Set-Up Row: K6, place marker, k378, place marker, k6.

Maintain garter st border on first and last 6 stitches of each row. The pattern stitch is presented in both written and charted form and is worked on the 378 sts between the markers. Following color sequence outlined on previous page, repeat pattern until entire color sequence has been worked three times. Bind off loosely.

Finishing

Use tapestry needle to weave in ends. Block.

Feather and Fan Lace Pattern

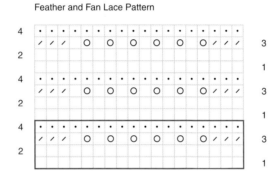

Maintain garter st border on first and last 6 stitches of each row.

Feather and Fan Triangle Shawl

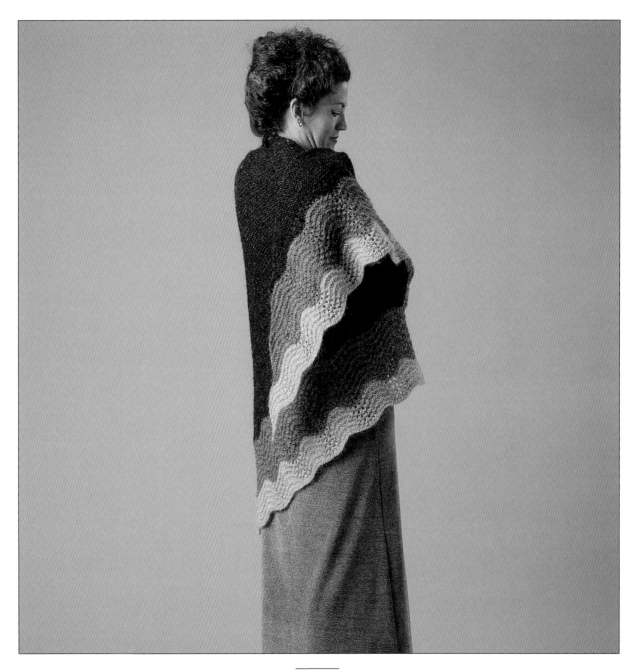

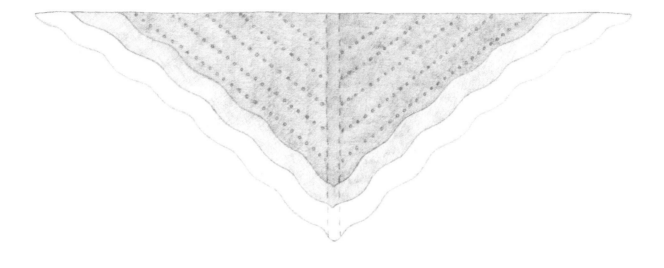

Feather and Fan Triangle Shawl

The Icelandic triangle has some special features. It is knitted from the top down beginning with only seven stitches. The triangle grows rapidly by increasing on each end and in the middle of the shawl on every other row. In addition, two rows near the top have extra shaping increases that help keep the shawl on the shoulders. About two-thirds of the way through the shawl, work the increases on each end on every row to create long elegant tails that you can wrap or tie many ways. The simple feather and fan stitch pattern creates a deep border and the bands of color provide the traditional Icelandic flavor. Because of the shawl's special shape, once the lace pattern begins, the instructions are presented only in charted form. If you haven't tried charts, now is your opportunity. Remember, if you want it, you can knit it!

Finished Size About 108" (274 cm) at top edge and 39" (99 cm) deep at point.

Yarn Unspun Icelandic wool; (100% wool; 300 yd [274 m]/3½ oz): black, 2 wheels; dark gray and silver gray, 1 wheel each.

Needle Size 8 (5 mm): 24" (60-cm) circular. Adjust needle size if necessary to obtain the correct gauge.

Notions Stitch markers; tapestry needle.

Gauge 16 sts and 24 rows = 4" (10 cm) in St st.

Note Slip markers on all rows.

Feather and Fan Triangle Lace Pattern

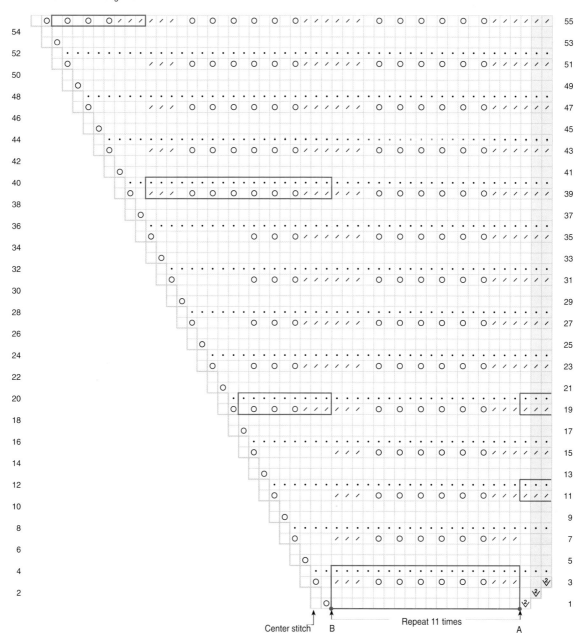

Center stitch   B   Repeat 11 times   A

Feather and Fan Triangle Lace Pattern

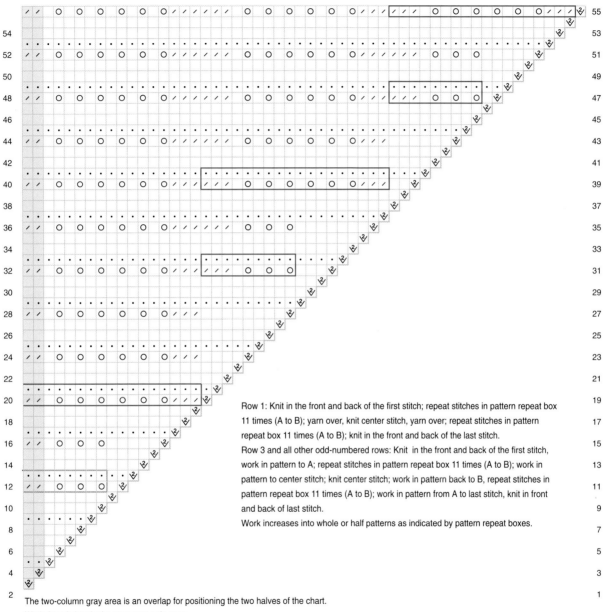

Row 1: Knit in the front and back of the first stitch; repeat stitches in pattern repeat box 11 times (A to B); yarn over, knit center stitch, yarn over; repeat stitches in pattern repeat box 11 times (A to B); knit in the front and back of the last stitch.

Row 3 and all other odd-numbered rows: Knit in the front and back of the first stitch, work in pattern to A; repeat stitches in pattern repeat box 11 times (A to B); work in pattern to center stitch; knit center stitch; work in pattern back to B, repeat stitches in pattern repeat box 11 times (A to B); work in pattern from A to last stitch, knit in front and back of last stitch.

Work increases into whole or half patterns as indicated by pattern repeat boxes.

The two-column gray area is an overlap for positioning the two halves of the chart.

Work the stitches in the gray area only once.

Shawl

Cast on 7 sts.

Row 1: Kfb, k2, yo, k1 (mark this center stitch), yo, k2, kfb—11 sts.

Row 2 and all even-numbered (WS) rows: Knit.

Row 3: Kfb, k4, yo, k1, yo, k4, kfb—15 sts.

Row 5: Kfb, k6, yo, k1, yo, k6, kfb—19 sts.

Row 7: Kfb, knit to center st, yo, k1, yo, knit to last st, kfb.

Row 8: Knit.

Rows 9–16: Repeat rows 7 and 8—39 sts.

Work eyelet row

Eyelet row: Kfb, *yo, k2tog; repeat from * to center st, yo, k1, yo, *k2tog, yo; repeat from last * to last st, kfb—43 sts.

Next 5 rows: Beginning with row 8, repeat rows 7 and 8—51 sts.

> *Repeat last 6 rows once—63 sts.*

Increase Row: Increase 8 sts evenly spaced between the beginning kfb and the yo before center st and between the yo after the center st and the ending kfb—83 sts.

Next 5 rows: Beginning with row 8, repeat rows 7 and 8—91 sts.

Increase row: Increase 11 sts evenly spaced on each side of center st—117 sts.

Next 5 rows: Beginning with row 8, repeat rows 7 and 8—125 sts.

Next row: Work eyelet row—129 sts.

Next 5 rows: Beginning with row 8, repeat rows 7 and 8—137 sts.

Next row: Work eyelet row—141 sts.

Next 35 rows: Beginning with row 8, repeat rows 7 and 8—209 sts.

Next row: Work eyelet row—213 sts.

Next 5 rows: Beginning with row 8, repeat rows 7 and 8—221 sts.

Next row: Work eyelet row—225 sts.

Next 17 rows: Beginning with row 8, repeat rows 7 and 8—257 sts.

Next row: Work eyelet row—261 sts.

Next 5 rows: Beginning with row 8, repeat rows 7 and 8—269 sts.

Next row: Work eyelet row—273 sts.

Tails

Row A (WS): Kfb, knit to last st, kfb.

Row B (RS): Kfb, knit to center st, yo, k1, yo, knit to last st, kfb.

Repeat rows A and B for 33 more rows—377 sts.

Next row: Work eyelet row—381 sts.

Repeat rows A and B for five rows—395 sts.

Next row: Work eyelet row—399 sts.

Begin lace pattern and color bands

On next row (WS), change to medium gray and purl one row. Begin feather and fan lace from charts. Continue to increase at each end on every row and on each side of the center stitch on every other row throughout the lace pattern. When charts are complete, knit one row. Bind off loosely in knit.

Finishing

Use tapestry needle to weave in ends. Block.

Seven

Victorian England

Wool Peddler's Shawl

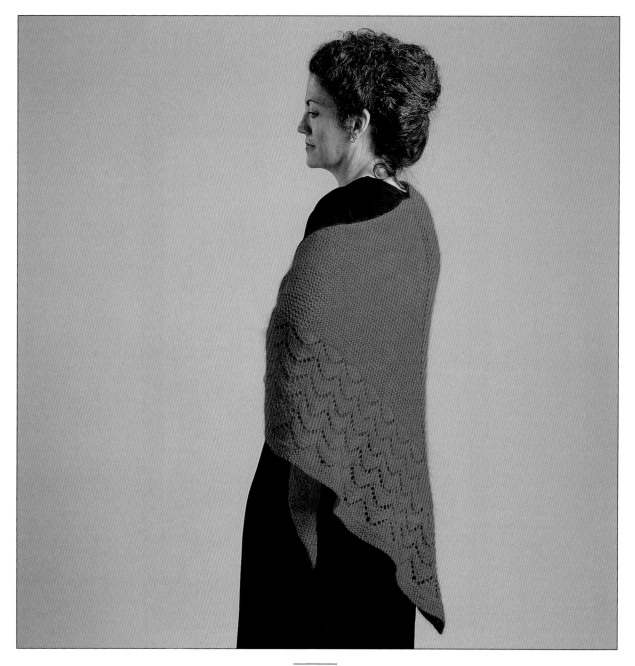

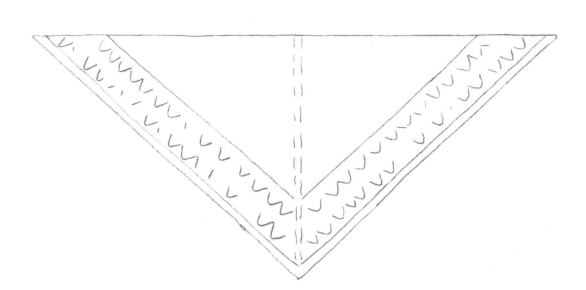

Wool Peddler's Shawl

On market days in eighteenth- and nineteenth-century Europe, itinerant peddlers roamed the marketplaces with baskets of their wares. Women who sold knitted stockings, mittens, and handspun yarns often wore bright red shawls to be recognized in the crowds. It became a fad in Victorian England to make peddler dolls, and the wool peddler doll was always wrapped in a pretty red shawl.

The Wool Peddler's shawl is triangular, worked from the top down in garter stitch to a traditional lace pattern with a garter-stitch border.

Finished Size About 78" (198 cm) wide at top edge and 34" (86 cm) deep at point.

Yarn Creative Yarns International Superkid Luxe (80% superfine kid mohair, 20% wool; 118 yds [108 m]/ 1¾ oz): #604, 7 skeins

Needle Size 7 (4.5 mm): 24" (60-cm) circular. Adjust needle size if necessary to obtain the correct gauge.

Notions Stitch markers; tapestry needle.

Gauge 16 sts and 24 rows = 4 (10 cm) in garter stitch.

Note All rows are charted for lace pattern. Slip markers on all rows.

Shawl

Cast on 7 sts.

Row 1 (RS): K1, yo, k2, yo, k1 (put a marker in this center stitch), yo, k2, yo, k1—11 sts.

Row 2 and all even-numbered rows: Knit.

Row 3: K1, yo, k4, yo, k1, yo, k4, yo, k1—15 sts.

Row 5: K1, yo, k6, yo, k1, yo, k6, yo, k1—19 sts.

Continue as above, making yarnovers after first st, before last st, and on each side of the center st every other row until 113 rows have been worked from beginning and ending on RS—231 sts on needle.

Begin Lace Pattern

Set-Up Row: Knit 4, place marker, p111, place marker,

Wool Peddler's Lace Chart – section 2

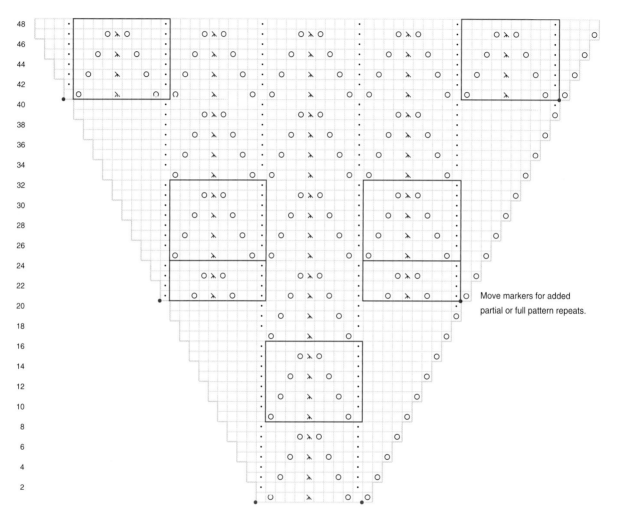

Move markers for added
partial or full pattern repeats.

Wool Peddler's Lace Chart – section 1

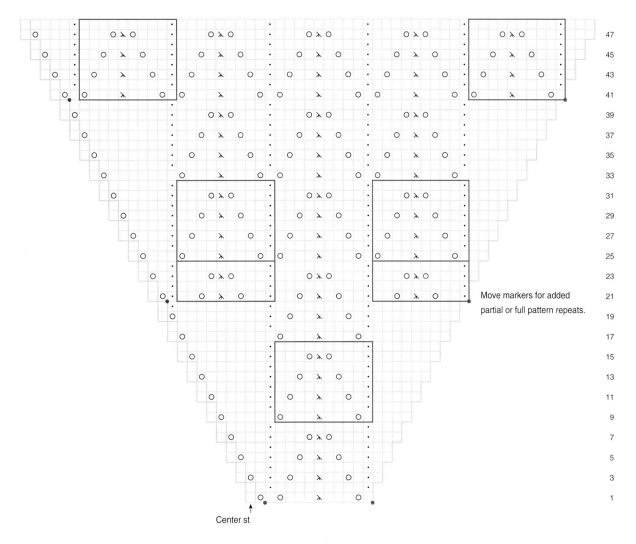

Move markers for added
partial or full pattern repeats.

Center st

p1, place marker, p111, place marker, k4.

Following lace chart or written instructions, work pattern between the markers in both large sections of shawl. Increases continue as before and are included in the row instructions. When you've increased 10 sts on the outsides of the markers, move them over 10 sts and add another repeat of the scallop lace pattern at both ends of the two large sections. The additions will occur on row 21 (row 13 of lace pattern) and on row 41 (row 9 of lace pattern).

Lace pattern (multiple of 10 sts plus 1)

Row 1: K1, yo, knit to marker, *k1, yo, k3, (sl 1, k2tog, psso), k3, yo; repeat from * to 1 st before next marker, k1, yo, knit center st, yo, repeat from * to 1 st before next marker, end k1, knit to last st, yo, k1.

Row 2 and all even-numbered rows: K4, purl to marker, *k1, p9; repeat from * to 1 st before next marker, k1, purl sts between next 2 markers, repeat from * to 1 st before next marker, k1, purl to last 4 sts, k4.

Row 3: K1, yo, knit to marker, *p1, k1, yo, k2, (sl 1, k2tog, psso), k2, yo, k1; repeat from * to 1 st before next marker, p1, knit to center st, yo, k1, yo, knit to next marker, repeat from * end p1, knit to last st, yo, k1.

Row 5: K1, yo, knit to marker, *p1, k2, yo, k1, (sl 1, k2tog, psso), k1, yo, k2; repeat from * to 1 st before next marker, p1, knit to center st, yo, k1, yo, knit to next marker, repeat from * end p1, knit to last st, yo, k1.

Row 7: K1, yo, knit to marker, *p1, k3, yo, (sl 1, k2tog, psso), yo, k3, repeat from * to 1 st before next marker, p1, knit to center st, yo, k1, yo, knit to next marker, repeat from * end p1, knit to last st, yo, k1.

Row 9: K1, yo, knit to marker, *k1, yo, k3, (sl 1, k2tog, psso), k3, yo; repeat from * to 1 st before next marker, knit to center st, yo, k1, yo, knit to next marker, repeat from * to 1 st before next marker, end knit to last st, yo, k1.

Row 11: K1, yo, knit to marker, *p1, k1, yo, k2, (sl 1, k2tog, psso), k2, yo, k1; repeat from * to 1 st before next marker, p1, knit to center st, yo, k1, yo, knit to next marker, repeat from * to 1 st before next marker, end p1, knit to last st, yo, k1.

Row 13: K1, yo, knit to marker, *p1, k2, yo, k1, (sl 1, k2tog, psso), k1, yo, k2; repeat from * to 1 st before next marker, p1, knit to center st, yo, k1, yo, knit to next marker, repeat from * to 1 st before next marker, end p1, knit to last st, yo, k1.

Row 15: K1, yo, knit to marker, *p1, k3, yo, (sl 1, k2tog, psso), yo, k3, repeat from * to 1 st before next marker, p1, knit to center st, yo, k1, yo, knit to next marker, repeat from * end p1, knit to last st, yo, k1.

Work rows 1–16 once, then work rows 9–16 four more times, moving pattern repeat markers as necessary.

Bottom border

Row 1: K1, yo, knit to center st, yo, k1, yo, knit to last st, yo, k1.

Row 2: Knit.

Repeat rows 1 and 2 three more times. Bind off loosely.

Finishing

Use tapestry needle to weave in ends. Block.

Eight

Russia

The **domovoi of** Russia were elf-like helpers whose specialty was domestic affairs. Every home and farm had a domovoi who was sometimes called "well-wisher." Domovoi were almost always invisible because they did not like to be noticed but went about their work quietly, protecting the home and helping the residents with their chores. Domovoi liked order and were especially helpful to the good housekeeper, sometimes even spinning or finishing the odd knitting project. Pity, however, the knitter who was slack in her housekeeping or who took to foul language, which the domovi deplored. An angry domovoi would roam the house at night, banging pots, swinging brooms, tangling yarn, and even poking the offender with her own knitting needles.

During a knitting class I was teaching, a woman came in with what looked like a silky cloud sticking out of her bag. In fact it was a handspun, handknitted shawl she'd just received from her daughter in Russia. While it was much simpler than an Orenburg lace shawl, it had an appeal of its own, and it was the inspiration for this design, a rectangular shawl with a simple pattern and a knitted-on lace border. The shawl is very long and can be wrapped around the head and shoulders. If you want a shorter shawl, work thirty pattern repeats instead of forty and pick up 300 sts instead of 360 sts on each long side for the border.

Domovoi Shawl

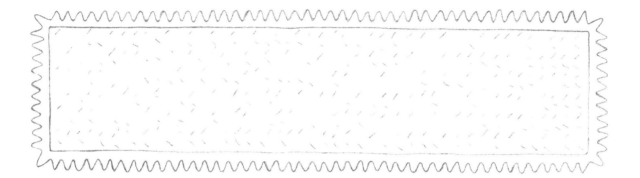

Domovoi Shawl

Finished Size About 102" (259 cm) long and 28" (71 cm) wide. (Shorter version is 78" [198 cm] long.)

Yarn Creative Yarns International Superkid Luxe (80% superfine mohair, 20% wool; 118 yd [108 m]/1¾ oz): #606, 11 skeins; 9 skeins for the shorter version.

Needle Size 10 (6 mm): 24" (60-cm) circular. Adjust needle size if necessary to obtain the correct gauge.

Notions Stitch markers; tapestry needle.

Gauge 12 sts and 24 rows = 4" (10 cm) in garter stitch.

Note Only right-side (odd-numbered) rows are charted. Wrong-side (even-numbered) rows are worked as follows: Sl 1, knit. Slip markers on all rows.

Shawl

Using an invisible cast-on method (see pages 11–12), cast on 67 sts. Throughout the lace pattern, slip the first stitch of each row as if to purl with yarn in front.

Lace pattern (multiple of 11 sts plus 13)

Set-up row (WS): Sl 1, knit to end, increasing 1 st—68 sts.

Row 1: Sl 1, k6, *yo, ssk, k9; repeat from *, end last repeat k4.

Row 2 and all even-numbered rows: Sl 1, knit.

Row 3: Sl 1, k6, *k1, yo, ssk, k8; repeat from *, end last repeat k3.

Row 5: Sl 1, k3, k2tog, yo, k1, *k2, yo, ssk, k4, k2tog, yo, k1; repeat from *, end k2, yo, ssk, k2.

Row 7: Sl 1, k2, k2tog, yo, k2, *k3, yo, ssk, k2, k2tog, yo, k2; repeat from *, end k3, yo, ssk, k1.

Row 9: Sl 1, k1, k2tog, yo, k3, *k6, k2tog, yo, k3; repeat from *, end k6.

Row 11: Sl 1, k2tog, yo, k4, *k5, k2tog, yo, k4; repeat from *, end k6.

Repeat rows 1–12 forty times, decreasing 1 stitch on the last row—67 sts. Do not bind off; do not break yarn. Put sts on a holder.

Set up for edging

With attached yarn, pick up by knitting (see page 15) 360 sts along the first long side of the stole as follows: pick up in 1 edge st, *make 1, pick up in next 2 edge sts; repeat from *, end make 1, pick up in 1 edge st.

Knit across the second short edge of invisibly cast-on sts and pick up by knitting 360 sts along second side. Put these 787 live sts on a piece of contrasting colored scrap yarn to hold them. You now have 854 total live stitches.

Lace edging

The edging is attached to the live sts of the shawl as it is knitted (see Knitted-On Borders on page 15). The only grafting is to join the beginning and end of the border. Beginning 1 st away from a corner of the shawl, work the last st of each even-numbered row of the border together with a st from the holder, using either ssk or k2tog. Just be sure to be consistent and use the same method throughout the attachment. See the special directions for the corners.

Cast on 6 sts invisibly.

Row 1: Sl 1, k1, yo, k2tog, yo, k2—7 sts.

Rows 2, 4, 6, and 8: Knit to last st, work the last st tog with a held shawl st.

Row 3: Sl 1, k2, yo, k2tog, yo, k2—8 sts.

Row 5: Sl 1, k3, yo, k2tog, yo, k2—9 sts.

Row 7: Sl 1, k4, yo, k2tog, yo, k2—10 sts.

Row 9: Sl 1, k5, yo, k2tog, yo, k2—11 sts.

Row 10: Bind off 5, knit to last st, work the last st tog with a held shawl st—6 sts.

Repeat 10-row pattern around all four sides of the shawl, working the corners as follows:

Corners

At each corner st, work 1 repeat of the edging as follows:

Row 1: Sl 1, k1, yo, k2tog, yo, k2.

Row 2: Knit to the last st, work the last st tog with corner st that is on hold from the shawl.

Row 3: Sl 1, k2, yo, k2tog, yo, k2.

Rows 4, 6, and 8: Knit to the last st, turn (do not knit the last st).

Row 5: K3, yo, k2tog, yo, k2.

Row 7: K4, yo, k2tog, yo, k2.

Row 9: K5, yo, k2tog, yo, k2.

Row 10: Bind off 5, knit to last st, work the last st tog with the same corner st worked at the beginning.

When the last corner is complete, use tapestry needle to graft the beginning and end of the edging together (see page 14).

Finishing

Use tapestry needle to weave in ends. Block.

Domovoi Lace Pattern

Row 2 and all even-numbered rows: Slip 1 as to purl with yarn in front, knit to end.

Domovoi Edging

Cast-on row

Nine

Scotland

There are many mermaid legends in the folklore of the British Isles. One tells of a mermaid who fell madly in love with a sailor on a ship headed for the Shetland Islands. Her ardor was so great that King Neptune granted her wish to trade her tail for legs. As she started ashore, the mermaid realized that she needed earthly clothes. She fashioned a shawl from sea foam and wore it as she stepped from the water. Of course the sailor was smitten and whisked her away to live happily ever after. Seeing the great beauty of the mermaid's shawl, the women of the island immediately took up their knitting needles and began to knit the now famous Shetland shawls to imitate the mermaid's sea-foam garment.

Shetland knitters created fabulous heirloom lace shawls that were prized by the upper classes in Victorian England. The knitters themselves usually wore a heavier and warmer shawl knitted from Shetland jumper-weight wool. Simple and beautiful lace patterns often adorned these shawls. The common lace patterns of Scotland are inspired by nature, as their names suggest: fir cones, crest of the wave, razor shell. They are also quite easy to memorize and knit.

Fir Cone Square Shawl

Fir Cone Square Shawl

The Fir Cone Square Shawl is constructed with almost no grafting. While this is not the traditional method, it makes knitting a Shetland-style shawl a real pleasure. The central square is knitted first in the traditional fir cone pattern. Fir cone is what is called a fully-fashioned lace because the decreases are worked in one place while the yarnovers are worked at another. This technique gives the lace fabric an interesting wavy effect. The large inner borders are picked up around the center square and knitted in the round. You create mitered corners by increasing with yarnovers on each side of the corner stitches every other row. The outer border is knitted onto the shawl once the inner borders are complete.

Finished Size About 63" (160 cm) square.

Yarn Harrisville Designs Shetland (100% wool; 900 yd [823 m]/8-oz cone): blueberry, 2,200 yd (2.012 m).

Needle Size 7 (4.5 mm): 24" (60-cm) circular. Adjust needle size if necessary to obtain the correct gauge.

Notions Stitch markers; tapestry needle; scrap yarn.

Gauge 16 sts and 24 rows = 4" (10 cm) in St st.

Note Only right-side (odd-numbered) rows are charted. Wrong-side (even-numbered) rows are purled. Slip markers on all rows.

Center square
Using an invisible cast-on method (see pages 11–12), cast on 153 sts. Purl 1 row.

Fir cone pattern (multiple of 10 sts plus 3)
Rows 1, 3, 5, and 7: Knit 2, *yo, k3, (sl 1, k2tog, psso),

k3, yo, k1; repeat from *, end last repeat k2.

Row 2 and all even-numbered row   Purl.

Rows 9, 11, 13, and 15: Knit 1, k2tog, *k3, yo, k1, yo, k3, (sl 1, k2tog, psso); repeat from *, end last repeat ssk, k1.

Repeat 16-row pattern 12 times and then work Rows 1–8 once more. Knit one more row. Do not break yarn. Place all sts on a piece of scrap yarn.

Inner border

The inner border that surrounds the center square is knitted in one piece on a circular needle. You will pick up stitches around the center square and join. Immediately after picking up the stitches, you will work a yarnover round to imitate the grafting rows on a traditional Shetland shawl. Two stitches will be marked off at each corner for the mitered corners and you'll knit the border, repeating the lace pattern on each of the four sides. There are two lace patterns for the inner border.

Pick up sts for inner border

Beginning at the corner where the yarn is attached and with the right side facing you, pick up by knitting (see page 15) 153 sts along the first selvedge edge of the shawl. The easiest way to do this is to pick up one st in every other row and add a st by doing a make one increase every 2 sts. In other words, pick up as follows: Pick up in 1 slipped st, *make 1, pick up in next 2 slipped sts; repeat from *, end make 1, pick up in 1 slipped st; repeat from * to corner—153 sts.

Knit across the invisibly cast-on sts—306 sts.

Repeat the pick up method used on the first side— 459 sts.

Knit sts from holder—612 sts: 153 sts on each side.

Marker round

Join into a round by knitting into the first picked-up stitch, place marker (make it a unique color to indicate beginning of round) [k151, place marker, k2, place marker] 3 times, k151, place marker, k2 (the last stitch of this k2 is the first joining stitch–yes, you will be knitting it twice on this round!). Each of the corners now have 2 sts between the markers. By increasing on each side of these marked corners with yarnovers, you will make the corners mitered as you knit the borders. Work 2 eyelet rounds as follows:

Eyelet rounds

Rnd 1: *Yo, k1, [yo, k2tog] to marker, yo, k2; repeat from *, end yo, k2.

Rnd 2: Knit—153 sts between markers.

Increase/miter round

Rnd 1: Yo, *knit to next marker, yo, k2, yo; repeat from *, end yo, k2.

Rnd 2: Knit—155 sts between markers.

Repeat rnds 1 and 2 once—157 sts between markers on each of the four sides of the inner border—636 sts.

Begin lace pattern

Note: Only odd-numbered rounds are charted. Even-numbered rnds are knitted. Slip markers on every round. Lace patterns are charted for ease in seeing how they fit into the increased sections.

Work increases every other round. Follow chart for Inner Border Lace Pattern 1. The yarnovers on the edge of the chart are corner increases.

After completing Inner Border Lace Pattern 1, you will have 173 sts on each side between the markers. Follow chart for Inner Border Lace Pattern 2. After completing Inner Border Lace Pattern 2, you will have 213 sts on each side between the markers.

Knit one plain rnd decreasing 1 st each side—212 sts each side. Do not bind off. Break yarn and put all sts on scrap yarn to hold.

Move markers

Move the corner markers over one stitch (away from the corner) on each side so that there are four stitches marked off at each corner.

Lace edging

Note: Be sure to check as you attach the edging that the right side of the edging is showing on the right side of the shawl. This means that the wrong side of the shawl will be facing you on attaching (even-numbered) rows and the right side of the shawl will be facing you on odd-numbered rows.

The edging is attached to the live stitches of the shawl as it is knitted (see Knitted on Borders on page 15). No grafting! You may work from the written instructions or the chart. Beginning with the first stitch after a corner marker, work the last stitch of each even-numbered row of edging together with a stitch from the inner border holder. When you reach the corners, stop at the marker. Work one whole repeat of the edging over the next four stitches, attaching the edging to three of the four corner stitches twice. This will ensure that your lace edging is centered on the corners and that it doesn't curl. Break the yarn leaving a 10-inch tail for grafting after you've completed the edging.

Cast on 13 sts invisibly (see pages 11–12).

Set-Up Row: K2, purl to the last 2 sts, k1, ssk the last st with 1 st from the inner border of shawl.

Row 1 (RS): Sl 1, k3, yo, k5, yo, k2tog, yo, k2—15 sts.

Row 2 and all even-numbered rows: K2, purl to the last 2 sts, k1, ssk last st with 1 st from inner border of shawl.

Row 3: Sl 1, k4, (sl 1, k2tog, psso), k2, [yo, k2tog] 2 times, k1—13 sts.

Row 5: Sl 1, k3, ssk, k2, [yo, k2tog] 2 times, k1—12 sts.

Row 7: Sl 1, k2, ssk, k2, [yo, k2tog] 2 times, k1—11 sts.

Row 9: Sl 1, k1, ssk, k2, [yo, k2tog] 2 times, k1—10 sts.

Row 11: Sl 1, ssk, k2, yo, k1, yo, k2tog, yo, k2—11 sts.

Row 13: Sl 1, [k3, yo] 2 times, k2tog, yo, k2—13 sts.

Repeat 14-row pattern. Remember at the corners you will attach the edging on the same stitch twice to 3 of the 4 corner stitches. Use a tapestry needle to graft or weave ends of edging together.

Finishing

Using tapestry needle, weave in ends. Block the shawl out to be as square as possible since that will affect the way it drapes when worn.

Fir Cone Square Shawl Center

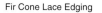

Row 2 and all even-numbered rows: purl.

Fir Cone Lace Edging

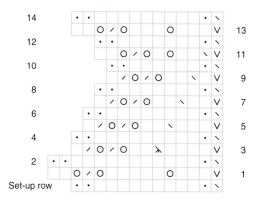

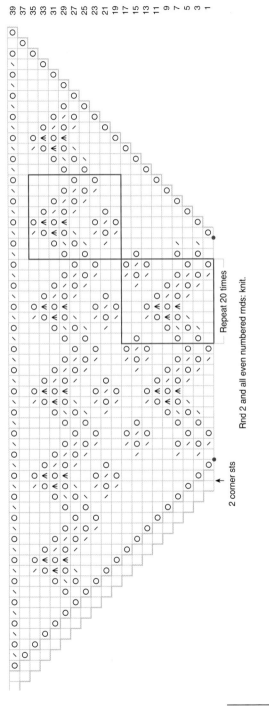

Fir Cone Square Inner Border Lace Pattern 2

39 37 35 33 31 29 27 25 23 21 19 17 15 13 11 9 7 5 3 1

Repeat 20 times

Rnd 2 and all even numbered rnds: knit.

2 corner sts

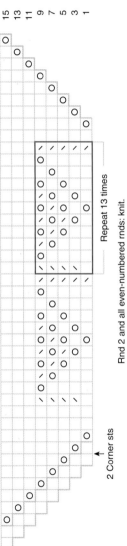

15 13 11 9 7 5 3 1

Repeat 13 times

Rnd 2 and all even-numbered rnds: knit.

Fir Cone Square Inner Border Lace Pattern 1

2 Corner sts

Highland Triangle Shawl

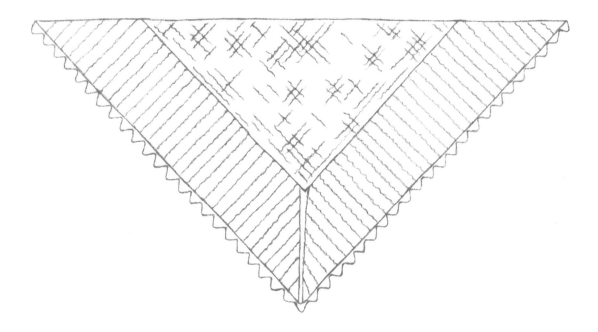

Highland Triangle Shawl

The Highland Triangle is constructed much like the Fir Cone Square. The center triangle is knitted first from tip to top. The inner borders are picked up on two sides of the triangle and knitted in one piece with a mitered corner. The outer border is a sideways edging that is knitted onto the shawl after the inner borders are complete.

Finished Size About 76" (193 cm) wide at the top edge and 39" (99 cm) deep at point.

Yarn Woolpak N.Z. 8 ply (100% wool; 525 yds [480 m/8¾ oz): tussock, 2 skeins.

Needle Size 8 (5 mm): 24" (60-cm) circular. Adjust needle size if necessary to obtain the correct gauge.

Notions Stitch markers; tapestry needle, scrap yarn.

Gauge 14 sts and 26 rows = 4" (10 cm) in garter stitch.

Note Only right-side (odd-numbered) rows are charted. Work wrong-side (even-numbered) rows as follows: Sl 1, m1, knit to end. Slip the first stitch of each row purl-wise with the yarn in front. Slip markers on all rows.

Shawl

Cast on 3 sts loosely.

Row 1: Sl 1, m1, k2.

Row 2: Sl 1, m1, knit to end.

Repeat row 2 until there are 10 sts on the needle.

Begin lace patterns

The lace patterns are charted for ease in seeing how they fit into the increased sections.

Following chart 1, work rows 7–48 once and then repeat rows 25–48 five more times. Knit 2 rows working increases as established—174 sts.

Work rows 169–172—176 sts.

Knit 4 rows working increases as established—180 sts, end on WS row. Bind off loosely. Do not break yarn.

Pick up stitches for inner borders

With the RS facing, begin at the corner where the yarn is attached and pick up by knitting (see page 15) 131 sts along the first selvedge edge of the shawl (from the top corner to the point). Pick up as follows: pick up in 1 st, *make 1, pick up in next 2 sts; repeat from * to corner, end make 1, pick up in 1 st. There should be 131 sts on the needle. Place a marker between the 130th and 131st stitch.

Pick up as for the first side, placing a marker between the 1st and 2nd stitch—262 sts. Maintain 2 center knit sts throughout. Turn and knit one row.

Eyelet pattern (RS)

Row 1: Sl 1, yo, k1, *yo, k2tog; repeat from * to marker, yo, k2, yo, **k2tog, yo; repeat from ** to last 2 sts, k1, yo, k1—132 sts on each side of center markers.

Row 2: (WS) Slip 1, m1, knit to end.

Row 3: Sl 1, m1, knit to marker, yo, k2, yo, knit to end—134 sts on each side of center markers.

Row 4: Slip 1, knit to end.

Begin lace pattern 2 (multiple of 6 sts plus 2)

Row 1: Sl 1, m1, k1, *yo, k1, (sl 2 tog kwise, k1, p2sso), k1, yo, k1; repeat from * to marker, yo, k2, yo; k1, **yo, k1, (sl 2, k1, p2sso), k1, yo, k1; repeat from ** end last rep k2.

Row 2: Sl 1, m1, knit to end.

Following chart for Lace Pattern 2, work rows 1–26 once and then rows 15–26 two times—184 sts on each side of the center markers ending on a WS row. Put all sts on scrap yarn to hold.

Lace edging

As the edging is knitted, it is attached to the live stitches of the shawl. Beginning with the first stitch of the inner border (top corner of first side), work the last stitch of each even-numbered row of the edging together with a stitch from the inner border holder. Use either ssk or k2tog to attach the borders. Just be sure to be consistent and use the same method throughout the attachment. **Note:** When you reach the point, stop at the first marker. You will be working one whole repeat of the edging over the next two stitches, which means you must attach the edging to the two corner stitches twice. This will ensure that your lace edging is centered on the point and that it doesn't curl.

Edging

Cast on 5 sts.

Row 1: Sl 1, k2, yo, k2—6 sts.

Row 2: K2, p1, k2, attach last st to shawl.

Row 3: Sl 1, k3, yo, k2—7 sts.

Row 4: K2, p1, k3, attach last st to shawl.

Row 5: Sl 1, k2, [yo] 2 times, k2tog, yo, k2—9 sts.

Row 6: K2, p1, k1, k1 into the first yo loop and p1 into the 2nd yo loop, k2, attach last st to shawl.

Row 7: Sl 1, k8—9 sts.

Row 8: BO 4 sts, k3, attach last st to shawl.

Repeat rows 1–8 for the pattern from the top corner to the point (see note above) and back up to the other top corner, ending with row 8.

Bind off loosely.

Finishing

Use tapestry needle to weave in ends. Block.

Highland Triangle Lace Pattern 1

171
169
47
45
43
41
39
37
35
33
31
29
27
25
23
21
19
17
15
13
11
9
7

Work rows 7–48 once, then highlighted rows 25–48 five more times—172 sts. Work rows 169–172—176 sts. Knit 4 rows working increases as established —180 sts. Bind off loosely.

Row 8 and all even-numbered rows: Slip 1 wyif, make 1, knit to end. Work increases into pattern as indicated by pattern repeat boxes.

Highland Triangle Edging

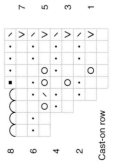

8
7
6
5
4
3
2
1
Cast-on row

Highland Triangle Lace Pattern 2

Section 2

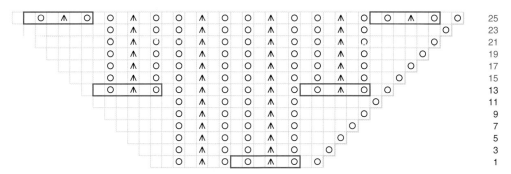

Section 1

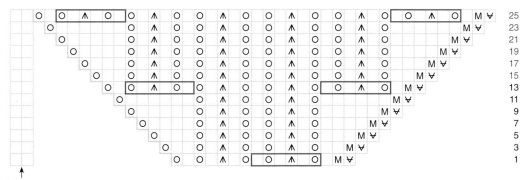

2 Center sts

Work row 1 of section 1, knit 2 center sts, followed by row 1 of section 2 once, then continue to work rows 2–26 in established pattern once; work highlighted rows 15–26 in established pattern two more times – 184 sts.

Row 2 and all even-numbered rows: Sl 1 pwise wyif, m1, knit to end.

Work increases into pattern as indicated by pattern repeat boxes.

North Sea Shawl

North Sea Shawl

The North Sea Shawl is constructed in the traditional manner and has two identical pieces on either side of a center panel. The first piece is knitted as one side, then continues through the center panel and is put on a holder. The second piece is knitted as the other side and is then grafted to the center panel.

Finished Size About 72" (183 cm) long and 22" (56 cm) wide.

Yarn Alice Starmore Scottish Campion (100% wool; 150 yds [137 m]/1 oz): scarlet, 8 skeins.

Needles Size 5 (3.75 mm): two 24" (60-cm) circulars. Adjust needle size if necessary to obtain the correct gauge.

Notions Stitch markers; tapestry needle, scrap yarn.

Gauge 18 sts and 28 rows = 4" (10 cm) in St st.

Note Slip markers on all rows.

Section 1
Cast on 109 sts. Knit 3 rows.

Lace pattern 1 (multiple of 12 sts plus 1)
Rows 1–4: Knit.
Row 5: K1, *[k2tog] 2 times, [yo, k1] 3 times, yo, [ssk] 2 times, k1; repeat from *.
Row 6: Purl.
Rows 7–12: Repeat rows 5 and 6.
Repeat these 12 rows fourteen times.

Lace pattern 2 (multiple of 2 sts plus 1)
Rows 1–4: Knit.
Row 5: K1, *yo, k2tog; repeat from *.

Rows 6 and 8: Knit.

Row 7: Purl.

Work rows 1-8 once.

Lace pattern 3 (Center Panel) (multiple of 12 sts plus 1)

Row 1: K1, *k3, k2tog, yo, k1, yo, ssk, k4; repeat from *.

Row 2 and all even-numbered (WS) rows: Purl.

Row 3: K1, *k2, k2tog, yo, k3, yo, ssk, k3; repeat from *.

Row 5: K1, *k1, [k2tog, yo] 2 times, k1, [yo, ssk] 2 times, k2; repeat from *.

Row 7: K1, *[k2tog, yo] 2 times, k3, [yo, ssk] 2 times, k1; repeat from *.

Row 9: K2tog, *yo, k2tog, yo, k5, yo, ssk, yo, (sl 1, k2tog, psso); repeat from * end last repeat ssk instead of (sl 1, k2tog, psso).

Row 11: K1, *k2tog, yo, k1, yo, ssk, k1; repeat from *.

Row 13: K2tog, *yo, k3, yo, (sl 1, k2tog, psso); repeat from *, end last repeat ssk instead of (sl 1, k2tog, psso).

Repeat rows 1–14 three times. Put sts on a scrap of yarn to hold.

Section 2

Cast on 109 sts and work as for section 1, ending on row 7 of lace pattern 2.

Finishing

Use tapestry needle to graft the two pieces together using stockinette Kitchener stitch (see page 14). Weave in ends. Block.

North Sea Shawl

Lace Pattern 3 – Center Panel

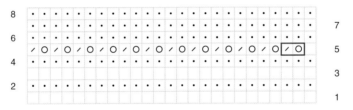

Lace Pattern 2

Lace Pattern 1

Ten

Mexico and South America

Textiles are part of many ancient rituals in Mexico and South America, while shawls and wraps are an intrinsic part of daily clothing. The *rebozo* developed from native clothing among the Indian and Mestizo population during Spanish rule. A simple rectangle, the rebozo is often made from wool or cotton in stripes of bright colors. Fringes are added, sometimes tied into intricate knotted patterns to represent good fortune. The rebozo is an all-purpose garment worn as a coat or headcovering, or used to hold a child or support a basket or jar that is carried on the head.

The *ruana* is a traditional South American garment. An elegant and stylish alternative to a coat, it is a classic favorite of weavers because it requires just two rectangles attached along the edge. There is no need to cut the precious woven fabric and there is no waste. The knitted ruana is styled after the classic woven garment.

The Rebozo

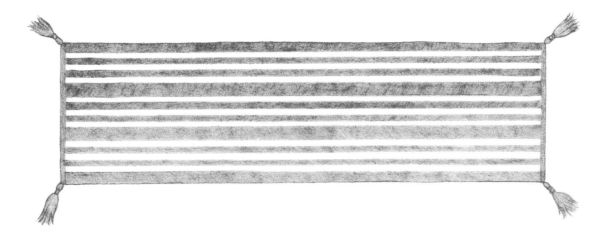

The Rebozo

Finished Size About 26" (66 cm) wide and 90" (229 cm) long.

Yarn Harrisville Designs Shetland (100% wool; 900 yd [823 m]/8-oz cone): black, 1,800 yd; magenta, russet, and violet, 300 yd each.

Needle Size 7 (4.5 mm): 32" (80-cm) circular and double-pointed. Adjust needle size if necessary to obtain the correct gauge.

Notions Stitch markers; tapestry needle.

Gauge 16 sts and 28 rows = 4" (10 cm) in garter st.

Shawl

With black, cast on 321 sts. Knit 6 rows and begin stripe pattern.

Stripe pattern

Rows 1–4: With black, knit.

Row 5: With black, *K2tog, yo; repeat from * to last st, k1.

Rows 6–10: With black, knit.

Rows 11–20: With magenta, repeat rows 1–10.

Rows 21–30: With black, repeat rows 1–10.

Rows 31–40: With russet, repeat rows 1–10.

Rows 41–50: With black, repeat rows 1–10.

Rows 51–60: With violet, repeat rows 1–10.

Rows 61–70: With black, repeat rows 1–10.

Rows 71–80: With black, knit.

Repeat rows 1–80 once, then rows 1–70 once. With black, knit 6 rows. Bind off loosely. Use tapestry needle to weave in ends. Block.

End borders and tassels

With right side facing and beginning at a corner, work a 5 st I-cord on the short ends of the rebozo attaching to every other row as follows.

I-cord

With double-pointed needles and black, cast on 5 sts. *Slide sts to other end of needle. Bringing yarn up across the back from the bottom st, k4, sl 1 pwise, pick up strand of yarn from edge of rebozo (between the garter ridges) with right-hand needle and ssk it tog with the last slipped st of I-cord. Repeat from * until you've completed the entire end of the shawl. Repeat on other short end.

Tassels (make 4)

Wrap black yarn 30 times around an 8" (20-cm) piece of cardboard. Cut one end and tie a 12" (30.5-cm) strand of yarn tightly around the middle of the tassel strands, tying the ends together. Leave the tails of the tying yarn intact.

Fold the tassel in half where it is tied and wrap a long strand several times around the whole tassel approximately one inch from the top. Secure ends of the wrap. Trim tassel to desired length and attach one to each corner of the shawl with the tails of the first tying strand.

Knitted Ruana

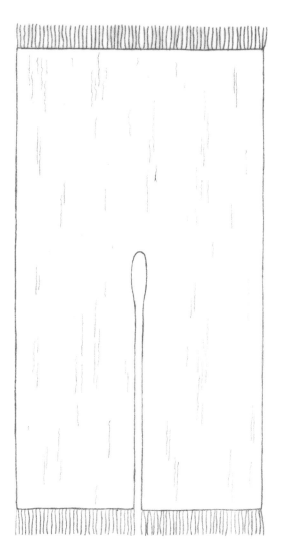

Knitted Ruana

This garment is knitted in garter stitch from side edge to side edge and is reversible. The fringes are made at the beginning and end of each row. The collar is worked last and gives this ruana a special fit. Traditional woven ruanas have a V opening at the back of the neck. This V leaves the back of your neck exposed to the wind and the point of the V is a stress point on the garment. Finishing the ruana with a collar reinforces the back for better wear and keeps the neck covered and cozy.

The length and width of the knitted ruana can be altered to make a custom fit. Instructions for alterations are included here.

Texture, Color, and Design

Use many different textures and weights of yarn: Wool, mohair, loop, chenille, worsted, bulky, or thick-and-thin yarns all work well together. Include novelty yarns for a bit of interest. Mohair is especially suitable to keep the ruana lightweight. Use fine yarns double. And by all means add some glitz!

When choosing yarn, decide whether you want a multicolored woven effect or a monochromatic tone-on-tone. You get a striped effect with yarn colors that contrast. You get a blended, woven effect with yarns that vary in tone but come from a similar color family. If you choose a blended fabric, do be sure to add a bit of interest by knitting a row here and there with a beautiful contrasting color.

Whether you use many different colors or many different tones, it's important to make a smooth gradual change from one color or tone to the next. For the best effect, make the change after knitting an odd number of rows; knit one or three or five rows of one yarn, then make a change. Remember that the ruana is knitted entirely in garter stitch and that it takes two rows of knitting to make one ridge in garter stitch. By knitting an odd number of rows of any one color before changing to a new color, you create a ridge that is a mixture of both colors. This two-color ridge makes a more gradual transition than does a straight-edge stripe. But beware of very strong contrast! If your change is dramatic, say from red to green, do several transition rows by alternating one row of each color for four to ten rows. This is also a wonderful way to mix yarn colors and create a completely new color stripe.

Do not worry about making the two halves of the ruana match stripe for stripe. The important issue is color balance. Use about the same amount of each color in each half of the ruana. If you have several stripes of one color in the first half, try to use about the same amount of that color in the second half.

Swatching will help you work out the best color mix and is also very important for determining the stitch gauge with a mixture of yarns. In the swatch, use as many as possible of the yarns you intend to use in the ruana. This is your opportunity to experiment with color choices and combinations.

You may also use the swatch to practice the cutting and tying techniques that produce the fringes at the ends of each row. Following the tying and knitting instructions, cast on 30 stitches and work in fringed garter stitch for 4". The swatch should measure 8½" (21.5 cm). Is it 8" (20 cm)? Go up a needle size. Is it 9" (23 cm)? Go down a needle size.

Keep your swatches and use them to practice washing and blocking as well as different methods of tying fringe.

Tying and knitting

To cast on, take two strands of yarn and tie them together with an overhand knot, leaving 14-inch (35.5cm) tails. Starting at the knot, proceed to cast on with the long-tail

method with one strand over the thumb and one strand over the index finger.

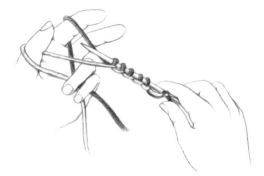

When all sts are cast on, leave 14-inch tails and cut both strands of yarn. Start the first row with a new single strand of yarn, measure a 14-inch tail, tie it onto the tail at the end of the cast-on row, and then knit the row. At the end of this row, cut the knitting yarn and leave a 14-inch tail. With the yarn for the next row, measure a 14-inch tail and tie it to the last row's tail. Knit the row. Repeat this process of measuring and tying at the beginning and end of each row; even on rows where the color does not change, cut the yarn to leave a tail that becomes the fringe. Be sure to measure the fringes with a ruler each time you cut to keep them even in length.

Alterations to width and/or length
Width

The ruana may easily be made narrower by working fewer rows before working the center row. Because the weight of the garment will cause the sides to drop, it is not advisable to try to make the garment any wider than 46" (117 cm) total width. The 46-inch width looks great on most folks!

Length

Alter the length of the ruana by casting on a different number of stitches than called for. To figure out how many stitches to cast on, measure from the point on the back of the leg where the fringes are to end, over the shoulder, and down the front to the desired finished length. This gives the total length of the front and the back together with the fringes. Now subtract two times the length of the finished fringe from the original measurement. Subtract another 4" to allow for the "growing" that the ruana will do. Multiply the adjusted length measurement by the stitch gauge (Do that swatch!) and the result is the number of stitches that you will cast on. The alteration formula below will lead you through the calculations.

Alteration formula

1. Desired length of both front and back including fringe _____ (A) inches/cm
2. Desired length of fringe _____ (B) inches (cm)
3. $2 \times B$ (total of front and back fringes)_____ (F) inches (cm)
4. A minus F (length of front and back minus fringe)_____ (C) inches (cm)
5. C minus 4 inches (to allow for "growth")_____ (D) inches (cm)
6. D × Stitch Gauge _____ – number of stitches to cast on

Finished Size As desired OR
Width from wrist to wrist: 46" (117 cm)
Length from top of shoulder: 45" (114 cm) (includes 10" [25 cm] of fringe)
Yarn Variety of yarns totaling 2,500 yards (2286 m). (Assuming that a ball of yarn has about 100 yards (91.5 m), you will need 25 balls of yarn.)
Needle Size 7 (4.5 mm): 24" or 32" (60-cm or 80-cm) circular. Adjust needle size if necessary to obtain the correct gauge.
Notions Stitch markers; tapestry needle, scrap yarn.

Gauge 14 sts and 28 rows = 4" (10 cm) in garter st

Note The fringe starts out about 14" (35.5 cm) long. After tying and trimming it will still be at least 10" (25.5 cm) long.

The weight of the ruana will cause it to "grow" approximately 2" (5 cm) in length. The pattern accommodates the drop and the finished measurement is the adjusted length. If you want your ruana to be a different length, see alteration formula at left

First half

Cast on 236 sts. Tying 14-inch (35.5-cm) tails together before starting each row, work in garter stitch until work measures 23" (58.5) from the cast-on edge.

Center Row: Scrap yarn is knitted into the center and will be removed later to make the front opening. Use a bright scrap yarn that contrasts highly with the body of the ruana so that it is easy to see when the time comes to remove it.

With scrap yarn, knit to 5" (12.5 cm) past the middle of the row (136 stitches or the number for your length). Turn and knit back with the scrap yarn to the beginning of the row. Cut the scrap yarn. The center row is complete.

Second half

With the ruana yarn, leave a 14-inch (35.5-cm) tail and continue making fringes and knitting in garter stitch as for first half. When ruana is 46" (117 cm) wide, bind off loosely. Elizabeth Zimmermann's Casting-On Casting-Off Method (see page 13) of bind-off makes a beautiful elastic edge that will look identical to the long-tail cast-on edge at the beginning of the ruana. Taking the stitches off the needle and putting them on a string makes this method easier.

Finishing

Front opening: Remove the scrap yarn from the center row by cutting the scrap yarn stitches. Beginning at the bottom of the ruana, pick up the open stitches from each front edge and put them on a piece of scrap yarn to hold them. Put each side on a separate piece.

Collar: Beginning at the center back, knit the collar back and forth out along the edges of the neck opening, gradually filling in the V of the back neck. At the end of each row, add two more stitches to the width by knitting one stitch from the yarn holder, then slipping and wrapping the next stitch on the holder. By wrapping the slipped stitch you avoid leaving a hole when you turn to knit the next row.

Pick up one stitch from the center of the neck opening and knit it. *Put the next two stitches from the string holder on the left-hand needle. Knit the first of these stitches, slip the second stitch to the right-hand needle, bring the yarn to the front, slip the stitch back to the left-hand needle, turn, knit to the end, and repeat from *.

Continue until there are 100 stitches on the needle or until the collar is the desired depth (8–10" [20–25.5 cm]) from the center back. The deeper the collar, the more it will behave like a shawl collar. Put the collar stitches on a piece of scrap yarn to hold them and try the ruana on to make sure you like the collar depth.

Happy? Then you may start at the bottom of the ruana and use the Casting-on Casting-off method to bind off all the front opening stitches, including the collar. Be sure to bind off loosely so the edges do not restrict the wonderful drape.

Fringes

Leave the fringes loose as they are, tie them into tassels, or knot them with macramé. Experiment with the fringes on your swatch to find the perfect fringe effect.

Blocking

Wash and block the ruana following the guidelines on pages 15–16. While fringes are wet, slap them against the edge of a table or sink to straighten and fluff them.

Eleven

Norway

All around the United States, you can find small towns with wonderful historical museums that tell the story of immigrant settlers. Mt. Horeb, Wisconsin, is famous for its Mustard Museum and for the carved wooden creatures that line the "Trollway." Among the exhibits about Scandinavian settlers in the Mt. Horeb Area Historic Museum are examples of knitted lace and Nordic sweaters and socks. One woven shawl from Norway has a lovely subtle pattern of blocks with centered dots. It is simple, yet elegant, worked in black, and was obviously a treasured garment. It inspired this Norwegian shawl, which is a square with a simple box-lace pattern and garter-stitch borders.

Box–Lace Shawl

Box-Lace Shawl

Finished Size About 60" (152.5 cm) square

Yarn Jamieson & Smith Shetland, (100% wool; 150 yd [137 m]/1-oz skein): dark plum, 14 skeins.

Needle Size 7 (4.5 mm): 24" (60-cm) circular. Adjust needle size if necessary to obtain the correct gauge.

Notions Stitch markers; tapestry needle.

Gauge 16 sts and 29 rows = 4" (10 cm) in garter st.

Note Slip markers on all rows. Work the lace pattern on the 236 sts between the markers.

Shawl

Cast on 248 sts loosely (see page 11). Place markers after the first 6 sts and before the last 6 sts to mark the side borders. These first and last 6 sts will be knitted on every row throughout the shawl. The lace pattern is presented in both written and charted form.

Garter-stitch border

Knit 12 rows for bottom garter-stitch border.

Lace pattern (multiple of 10 sts plus 6)

Row 1 (RS): K2, *yo, k2tog; repeat from * to 2 sts before the last marker, k2.

Rows 2, 5 and 6: Knit.

Rows 3 and 7: K1, k2tog, yo, ssk, k1, *k5, k2tog, yo, ssk, k1; repeat from *.

Rows 4 and 8: *K2, (k1, p1) into the yo of previous row, k6; repeat from * end last repeat k2.

Row 9: K6, *k2tog, yo, ssk, k6; repeat from *.

Row 10: *K7, (k1, p1) into the yo of previous row, k1; repeat from * to 6 sts before last marker, k6.

Rows 11–16: Repeat rows 3–8 once.

Repeat 16-row pattern 25 more times, then work row 1 once more.

Garter-stitch border

Knit 12 rows for top garter-stitch border.

Finishing

Bind off very loosely. Use tapestry needle to weave in ends. Block.

Box-Lace Shawl Lace Pattern

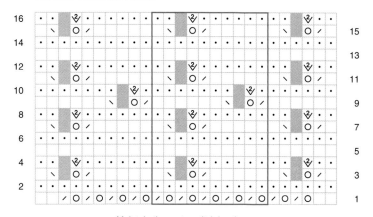

Maintain the garter stitch borders on
the first 6 and last 6 sts of each row.
Repeat Rows 1–16 twenty-six times.

Twelve

Native America

A powwow is a multidimensional event. It is a social gathering where new and old friends meet, a cultural event, and a religious occasion. A powwow also offers the opportunity for musicians and dancers to express themselves in the creative venue of traditional dances.

A child may choose a dance at a young age or the dance may be handed down from generation to generation. A dancer usually keeps the same dance throughout life. Choosing a dance is a rite of passage that begins the spiritual and social journey to adulthood. A shawl is an intrinsic part of women's fancy dancing. Among those done at powwows, the butterfly dance represents the story of a woman who after a long period of mourning has again embraced life and emerges like a butterfly from a cocoon to celebrate the joy and beauty of being alive. The butterfly shawl is usually made from cotton or a similar fiber that has a flowing drape. It is decorated, often beaded, always fringed.

Butterfly Shawl

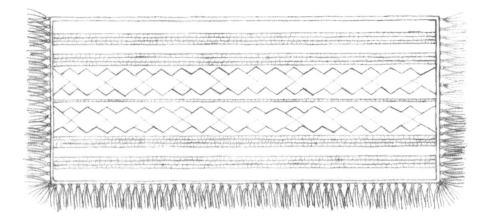

Butterfly Shawl

Finished Size About 72" (183 cm) long and 30 ½" (77.5 cm) wide.

Yarn Tahki Cotton Classic (100% cotton; 108 yd [99 m]/ 1¾ oz]): color # 3003, 18 skeins.

Needles Size 5 (3.75 mm): 24" or 32" (60-cm or 80-cm) circular. Border: Size 4 (3.5 mm): 24" or 32" (60-cm or 80-cm) circular. Adjust needle size if necessary to obtain the correct gauge.

Notions Stitch markers; tapestry needle.

Gauge 20 sts and 24 rows = 4" (10 cm) in St st.

Note All rows are charted. Slip markers on all rows.

Stitch patterns

Pattern #1

Row 1 (RS): *K2tog, yo, k2, repeat from *.

Row 2: *P2tog, yo, p2, repeat from *

Pattern #2

Row 1 (RS): Knit.

Row 2: Purl.

Pattern #3

Row 1: K5, [yo, ssk] 2 times, k3, [k2tog, yo] 2 times, k6.

Row 2 and all even-numbered (WS) rows: Purl.

Row 3: K3, [k2tog, yo] 2 times, k4, [k2tog, yo] 2 times, k1, yo, ssk, k4.

Row 5: K2, [k2tog, yo] 2 times, k4, [k2tog, yo] 2 times, k1, [yo, ssk] 2 times, k3.

Row 7: K1, [k2tog, yo] 2 times, k4, [k2tog, yo] 2 times, k3, [yo, ssk] 2 times, k2.

Row 9: K3, [yo, ssk] 2 times, k1, [k2tog, yo] 2 times, k5, [yo, ssk] 2 times, k1.

Row 11: K4, yo, ssk, yo, (sl 1, k2tog, psso), yo, k2tog, yo, k4, [k2tog, yo] 2 times, k3.

Row 13: K5, yo, ssk, yo, (sl 1, k2tog, psso), yo, k4, [k2tog, yo] 2 times, k4.

Row 15: K6, [yo, ssk] 2 times, k3, [k2tog, yo] 2 times, k5.

Row 17: K4, k2tog, yo, k1, [yo, ssk] 2 times, k4, [yo, ssk] 2 times, k3.

Row 19: K3, [k2tog, yo] 2 times, k1, [yo, ssk] 2 times, k4, [yo, ssk] 2 times, k2.

Row 21: K2, [k2tog, yo] 2 times, k3, [yo, ssk] 2 times, k4, [yo, ssk] 2 times, k1.

Row 23: K1, [k2tog, yo] 2 times, k5, [yo, ssk] 2 times, k1, [k2tog, yo] 2 times, k3.

Row 25: K3, [yo, ssk] 2 times, k4, yo, ssk, yo, k3tog, yo, k2tog, yo, k4.

Row 27: K4, [yo, ssk] 2 times, k4, yo, k3tog, yo, k2tog, yo, k5.

Shawl

With smaller needle, cast on 153 sts loosely (see page 11).

Bottom border

Row 1: *K2 tog, yo, repeat from * to last st, k1.

Rows 2–5: Knit, decreasing 1 st in the last row—152 sts.

Set-up Row: Change to the larger needle and work in pattern as follows:

Pattern #1 on first 4 sts, [Pattern #2 on next 12 sts, Pattern #1 on next 12 sts] two times, Pattern #3 on next 22 sts, Pattern #1 on next 4 sts, Pattern #3 on next 22 sts, Pattern #1 on next 12 sts, Pattern #2 on next 12 sts, Pattern #1 on next 12 sts, Pattern #2 on next 12 sts, Pattern #1 on last 4 sts.

Work in pattern sequence as set until you've completed 15 repeats of Pattern #3.

Top border

Rows 1–4: Knit, increasing 1 st in the last row—153 sts.

Row 5: *K2tog, yo, repeat from * to last st, k1.

Bind off loosely in knit.

Fringe

Traditionally, fringe is added to the ends and the bottom edge of the butterfly shawl. Cut strands 16" (40.5 cm) long. Fold four strands in half and, beginning at the first yarnover at the top edge, loop four folded strands through every other yarnover on one end. Attach an extra fringe at the yarnover at the bottom corner, and in every other yarnover across the bottom edge. Attach an extra fringe at the yarnover at the second bottom corner, and attach a fringe to every other yarnover along the end up to the top edge. Trim to 6" (15 cm) or desired length.

Finishing

Use tapestry needle to weave in ends. Block.

Butterfly Shawl

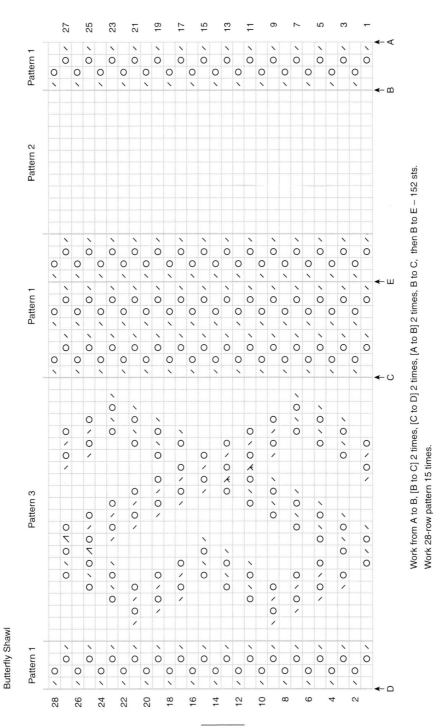

Work from A to B, [B to C] 2 times, [C to D] 2 times, [A to B] 2 times, B to C, then B to E – 152 sts.

Work 28-row pattern 15 times.

Thirteen

The Himalayas

In the Himalayan Mountains between Tibet and India, Cashmere goats are raised for their fine fleece. The poor men of the villages collect abandoned birds' nests that have been lined with bits of cashmere. The women sit for hours picking the cashmere from the nests and hand spinning exquisitely fine yarn. Then they weave this yarn into wonderful prayer shawls that are light as a feather and possess a truly magical and comforting quality. Here is a knitted version of this shawl.

Bird's Nest Shawl

Bird's Nest Shawl

This is a rectangular shawl with a simple lace pattern and garter-stitch borders.

Finished Size About 80" (203 cm) long and 21" (53.5 cm) wide.

Yarn Cashmere America 2 ply (100% cashmere; 437 yds [399.5 m]/1¾ oz): natural light brown, 6 skeins.

Needles Size 6 (4 mm): 24" (60-cm) circular. Size 5 (3.75 mm): 24" (60-cm) circular. Adjust needle size if necessary to obtain the correct gauge.

Notions Stitch markers; tapestry needle.

Gauge 18 sts and 24 rows = 4" (10 cm) in St st on larger needles.

Note Only right-side (odd-numbered) rows are charted. Wrong-side (even-numbered) rows are purled. Slip markers on all rows. Yarn is used doubled throughout.

Shawl

Note: Yarn is used doubled throughout.

With smaller needle, cast on 346 sts, knit 12 rows. Change to larger needle and place markers after the first 7 sts and before the last 7 sts. Work the pattern on the 332 sts between the markers. The first and last 7 sts will be knitted on every row throughout the shawl. The lace patterns are presented in both written and charted form.

Pattern Stitch (multiple of 11 sts plus 2)

Rows 1, 3, and 5: Knit.

Row 2 and all even-numbered rows: Purl.

Row 7: K1, *ssk, k4, yo, k5; repeat from * to 1 st before last marker, k1.

Row 9: K1, *ssk, k3, yo, k1, yo, k3, k2tog; repeat from * to 1 st before last marker, k1.

Row 11: K1, *ssk, k2, yo, k1, yo, ssk, yo, k2, k2tog; repeat from * to 1 st before last marker, k1.

Row 13: K1, *ssk, [k1, yo] 2 times, [ssk, yo] 2 times, k1, k2tog; repeat from * to 1 st before last marker, k1.

Row 15: K1, *ssk, yo, k1, yo, [ssk, yo] 3 times, k2tog;
  repeat from * to 1 st before last marker, k1.
Rows 17–26: Repeat Rows 7–16.
Rows 27–34: Work in St st.
Rows 35–44: Repeat rows 7–16.
Rows 45–46: Repeat rows 1–2.
  Repeat rows 1–46 three times.
  Repeat rows 1–4.

Top border

Switch to smaller needle and knit 12 rows.

Finishing

Bind off loosely. Use tapestry needle to weave in ends.
Block.

Bird's Nest Lace Pattern

Maintain the garter st borders on the first 7 and last 7 sts of each row.
Row 2 and all even-numbered rows: k7, purl to last 7 sts, k7.

Fourteen

Spain

Every culture holds the act of naming a child sacred. The naming ceremony not only establishes the child as a member of a particular faith, but welcomes the child into the family and the community. In many cultures, the act of naming occurs with the child's first meal, ensuring that the child will always be recognized and welcomed to the table for nourishment of body and soul.

The Spanish Christening Shawl was inspired by the one in the photograph on page 7 depicting a child on the way to be christened. The emotions and pride of the grandmother and sister are clear. In this case, the picture is truly worth a thousand words.

Spanish Christening Shawl

Spanish Christening Shawl

This is a square shawl with a simple diamond pattern and garter-stitch lace borders.

Finished Size About 60" (152.5 cm) square.

Yarn Henry's Attic Monty 3/9's (100% wool, 840 yd [768 m]/8-oz hank): natural, 3 hanks.

Needle Size 8 (5 mm): 24" (60-cm) circular. Adjust needle size if necessary to obtain the correct gauge.

Notions Stitch markers; tapestry needle; scrap yarn.

Gauge 14 sts and 20 rows = 4" (10 cm) in St st, very loosely knit.

Note Only right-side (odd-numbered) rows are charted. Work all wrong-side (even-numbered) rows as follows: Sl 1 pwise wyif, purl to end. Slip markers on all rows.

Shawl

Cast on 195 sts. Begin lace pattern. Throughout the lace pattern, slip first st pwise wyif.

Lace pattern

Row 1: Sl 1, k1, *k1, k2tog, yo, k1, yo, ssk, k2; repeat from *, end last repeat k3.

Row 2 and all even-numbered (WS) Rows: Sl 1, purl.

Row 3: Sl 1, k1, *k2tog, yo, k3, yo, ssk, k1; repeat from *, end last repeat k2.

Row 5: Sl 1, k2tog, *yo, k5, yo, (slip 1, k2tog, psso); repeat from *, end last repeat ssk, k1.

Row 7: Sl 1, k1, *yo, ssk, k3, k2tog, yo, k1; repeat from *, end last repeat k2.

Row 9: Sl 1, k1, *k1, yo, ssk, k1, k2tog, yo, k2; repeat from *, end last repeat k3.

Row 11: Sl 1, k1, *k2, yo, (slip 1, k2tog, psso), yo, k3; repeat from *, end last repeat k4.

Repeat 12-row pattern 28 times for the center of the shawl. Repeat row 1 once. Do not break yarn. Do not bind off.

Set-up for edging

Pick up by knitting (see page 15) 1 stitch in each of the slipped sts along the first side, increasing 29 sts evenly spaced as follows: *Pick up in 3 slipped sts, make 1, pick up 3 slipped sts, repeat from * until there are 197 sts picked up along the side, placing a marker in the first and last picked-up sts to mark corners; pick up 195 sts along the cast-on edge of shawl; pick up 197 sts along last side of shawl in same manner as the first side, again marking corners—784 sts. Join.

Rnd 1: *K2tog, yo; repeat from *.

Rnd 2: Knit.

Put all sts on a piece of yarn to hold them.

Lace edging

The edging is attached to the shawl as it is knitted (see Knitted-On Borders on page 15)—the only grafting nec-essary is to join the beginning and end of the border. Beginning one stitch after a corner of the shawl, work the last stitch of each even-numbered row of the edging together with a stitch from the holder. Use either ssk or k2tog to attach the borders. Just be sure to be consis-tent and use the same method throughout the attachment.

Note: The wrong side of the shawl will be facing you on attaching (even-numbered) rows and the right side of the shawl will be facing you on odd-numbered rows. This will make sense when you try it.

Cast on 20 sts invisibly (see pages 11–12).

Set-up row: Knit to last st, work last st tog with a held shawl st.

Row 1: Sl 1, k3, [yo, k2tog] 7 times, yo, k2—21 sts.

Rows 2, 4, 6, and 8: Knit to last st, work last st tog with a held shawl st.

Row 3: Sl 1, k6, [yo, k2tog] 6 times, yo, k2—22 sts.

Row 5: Sl 1, k9, [yo, k2tog] 5 times, yo, k2—23 sts.

Row 7: Sl 1, k12, [yo, k2tog] 4 times, yo, k2—24 sts.

Row 9: Sl 1, k23.

Row 10: Bind off 4, k18, work the last st tog with a st that is on hold from the shawl—20 sts.

Repeat rows 1–10 around all four sides of the shawl working one whole repeat of the edging in each corner st as follows:

Row 1: Sl 1, k3, [yo, k2tog] 7 times, yo, k2.

Row 2: Knit to the last stitch, work the last st tog with the corner st that is on hold from the shawl.

Row 3: Sl 1, k6, [yo, k2tog] 6 times, yo, k2.

Rows 4, 6, and 8: Knit to the last stitch, turn (do not knit the last st) and work the next row.

Row 5: K9, [yo, k2tog] 5 times, yo, k2.

Row 7: K12, [yo, k2tog] 4 times, yo, k2.

Row 9: K23.

Row 10: Bind off 4, knit to the last st, work the last st tog with the same corner st as on row 2.

Finishing

Use tapestry needle to graft lace border together with Kitchner stitch (see page 14) and weave in ends. Block.

Spanish Christening Lace Pattern

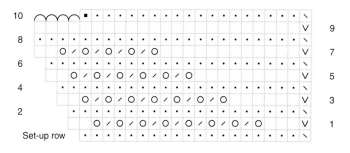

Row 2 and all even-numbered rows: slip 1 purlwise wyif, purl to end. Work rows 1–24 fourteen times, then work row 1 once more.

Spanish Christening Lace Edging

Fifteen

Variations

Sampler Shawl

The shawls in this chapter found their inspiration along the way as I was writing this book. The Sampler Shawl comes from the project in a class that I teach. The Sarah Blanch Shawl is a tribute to my grandmother's love of needlework, one that she passed on to me. The Basic Black shawl is based on the ubiquitous dark shawl that I found in many cultures around the world.

Sampler Shawl

Before there were pattern books, lace stitches were recorded in beautifully knitted samplers that were passed from knitter to knitter.

There are five basic lace patterns in this shawl. Because the pattern-repeat multiples differ from pattern to pattern, the number of stitches will occasionally be adjusted in the garter-stitch rounds between patterns or in the first round of the pattern. If you want a wider shawl, simply add a repeat or two of any pattern.

Finished Size About 86" (218.5 cm) long and 18" (46 cm) wide.

Yarn Alice Starmore Scottish Campion (100% wool, 150 yd [137 m]/1 oz):natural, 9 skeins.

Needle Size 6 (4 mm): 29" (80-cm) circular. Adjust needle size if necessary to obtain the correct gauge.

Notions Stitch markers; tapestry needle.

Gauge 20 sts and 30 rows = 4" (10 cm) in St st.

Note Slip markers on all rows.

Shawl

Cast on 401 sts loosely (see page 11). Place markers after the first 4 sts and before the last 4 sts to mark the garter stitch borders. These stitches will be knitted on every row throughout the shawl. The lace patterns are presented in both written and charted form and are worked on the sts between the markers.

Garter-stitch eyelet border

Rows 1–4: Knit.

Row 5: K1, *yo, k2tog; repeat from *.
Row 6: Knit.
Row 7: *K2tog, yo; repeat from *, end k1.
Row 8: Knit.

Pattern #1 (multiple of 14 sts + 1)
Rows 1, 3, 5, 7, and 9: K1 *yo, k3, ssk, yo, (sl 1, k2tog, psso), yo, k2tog, k3, yo, k1; repeat from *.
Rows 2, 4, 6, and 8: Purl.
Row 10: Knit.
Rows 11 and 12: Purl.
    Work 12-row pattern two times, decreasing 2 sts evenly spaced on last row—399 sts.

Pattern #2 (multiple of 6 sts + 1)
Row 1: K1, *yo, ssk, k1, k2tog, yo, k1; repeat from *.
Row 2 and all even-numbered rows: Purl.
Row 3: K1, *yo, k1, (sl 1, k2tog, psso), k1, yo, k1; repeat from *.
Row 5: K1, *k2tog, yo, k1, yo, ssk, k1; repeat from *.
Row 7: K2tog, *[k1, yo] 2 times, k1, (sl 1, k2tog, psso); repeat from * to the last 5 sts before the marker, [k1, yo] 2 times, k1, ssk.
    Work 8-row pattern three times.
    Knit 4 rows.

Pattern #3 (multiple of 10 sts + 1)
Rows 1, 3, 5, and 7: K1, *yo, k3, (sl 1, k2tog, psso), k3, yo, k1; repeat from *.
Row 2 and all even-numbered rows: Purl.
Rows 9, 11, 13, and 15: K2tog, *k3, yo, k1, yo, k3, (sl 1, k2tog, psso); repeat from *, end ssk.
    Work 16-row pattern two times.

Knit 4 rows, increasing 1 st on the last row—400 sts.

Pattern #4 (multiple of 4)
Row 1: *K2, yo, ssk; repeat from *.
Row 2: *P2, yo, p2tog; repeat from *.
Row 3: Repeat row 1.
Row 4: Repeat row 2.
    Work 4-row pattern three times.

Knit 4 rows, decreasing 1 st on the last row—399 sts.

Pattern #5 (multiple of 6 sts + 1)
    Rows 1, 3, and 5: K1, *yo, ssk, k1, k2tog, yo, k1; repeat from *.
    Row 2 and all even-numbered (WS) rnds: Purl.
    Row 7: K1, *k1, yo, (sl 1, k2tog, psso), yo, k2; repeat from *.
    Row 9: K1, *k2tog, yo, k1, yo, ssk, k1; repeat from *.
    Row 11: K2tog, *yo, k3, yo, (sl 1, k2tog, psso); repeat from *, end ssk.
    Work 12-row pattern two times.

Edging
    Rows 1–4: Knit increasing 2 sts evenly spaced on last row—401 sts.
    Row 5: K1, *yo, k2tog; repeat from *.
    Row 6: Knit.
    Row 7: *K2tog, yo; repeat from *, end k1.
    Rows 8–11: Knit. Bind off loosely.

Finishing
Use tapestry needle to weave in ends. Block.

Sampler Shawl Lace Patterns

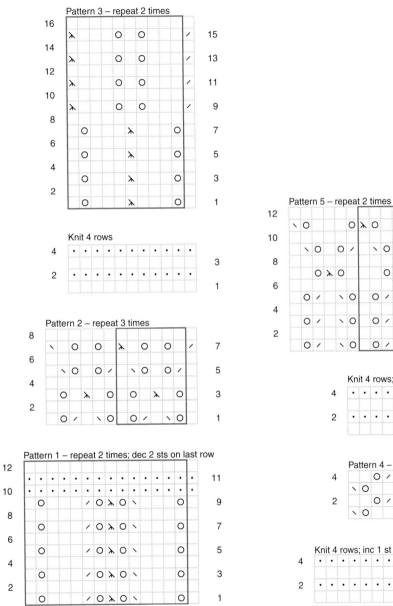

Maintain the garter stitch borders on the first 4 and last 4 stitches of each row.

Sarah Blanch Shawl

Sarah Blanch Shawl

At the age of ten, while visiting Grandma Ramsey, I pointed out a magazine photograph of a lady wearing a beautiful shawl. Sarah Blanch Ramsey, my maternal grandmother, decided she would make me a similar shawl. She was a hard-working, quiet woman who was adept at many forms of needlework. She had a hairpin lace loom and together we chose the yarn in a beautiful soft gold color. Grandma made the shawl on her loom in about three days. It was warm and wonderful, and I felt very elegant wearing it. This was the first real shawl I owned. The Sarah Blanch Shawl is very fast to knit and somewhat resembles hairpin lace. Rectangular, it uses a garter drop stitch.

Finished Size About 80" (203 cm) long and 22" (56 cm) wide.

Yarn Cheryl Oberle Designs Dancing Colors (50% merino, 50% mohair; 425 yd [389 m]/8-oz hank): evening, 2 hanks.

Needle Size 7 (4.5 mm): 24" (60-cm) circular. Adjust needle size if necessary to obtain the correct gauge.

Notions Tapestry needle.

Gauge 12 sts and 24 rows = 4" (10 cm) in garter st.

Garter drop pattern

Rows 1–6: Knit.

Row 7: Knit, wrapping the yarn around the needle 3 times after entering each stitch.

Row 8: Knit, dropping the extra wraps on each stitch.

Row 9–10: Knit.

Row 11: Knit, wrapping the yarn around the needle 3 times after entering each stitch.

Row 12: Knit, dropping the extra wraps on each stitch.

Tips for using hand-painted yarn

Because hand-painted yarn is dyed one skein at a time, color variations among skeins of the same color are part of the process and add to the beauty of the finished garment. To get the most homogeneous coloring pattern, wind each hank into two approximately equal balls and work with balls from alternate hanks throughout the knitting.

Shawl

Using a very flexible method (see page 11), cast on 240 sts loosely. Work in garter drop pattern, repeating pattern rows 1–12 eight times, then work rows 1–6 once more. Bind off loosely (use a needle two sizes larger to achieve a smooth and loose bind-off).

Finishing

Use tapestry needle to weave in ends. Block.

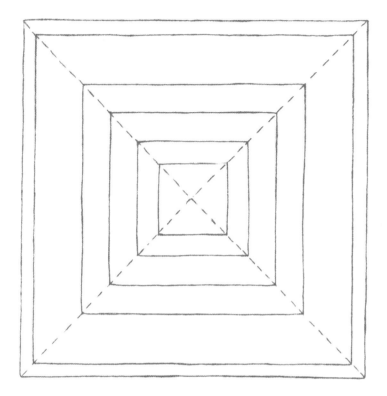

Basic Black Shawl

The basic black shawl is seen in many European countries. It's usually a square folded and worn as a triangle. In earlier times it could indicate social status as a married woman or a widow. Today it is often worn for its practicality: black goes with everything and absorbs the heat of the sun. However, this shawl is lovely in any color.

Finished Size About 60" (152.5 cm) square.

Yarn Harrisville Designs Shetland (100% wool; 900 yd [823 m]/8-oz cone): black, 2,200 yd (2,012 m).

Needles Size 7 (4.5 mm): double pointed, 16" (40 cm), and 29" (80-cm) circular. Adjust needle size if necessary to obtain the correct gauge.

Notions Stitch markers; tapestry needle.

Gauge 18 sts and 28 rows = 4" (10 cm) in St st.

Note Slip markers on all rnds. The shawl is started with a circular beginning that is easy to work and draws up into a beautifully tight center once enough stitches have been increased. Start with double-pointed needles and graduate to the 16" and then the 29" needle when the knitting gets too crowded on the shorter needle. Mark the indicated corner stitches with safety pins or split ring markers so that the markers move along with the knitting. After several rows it is easy to see where the marked corner stitches are; eliminate markers if desired.

Basic Black Shawl

Shawl

Using the modified circular start (see page 12), cast on 8 sts. Divide onto four dpn—2 sts per needle. Join and work as follows:

Rnd 1: *K1, yo; repeat from *—16 sts.

Rnd 2: Knit.

Rnd 3: [K1 (mark this st), yo, k3, yo] 4 times—24 sts.

The marked stitches are the corner stitches, and the yarnover increases are worked on either side of these stitches on every other round throughout the shawl. Mark the first stitch with a uniquely colored marker to indicate the beginning of the round.

Rnd 4 and all even-numbered rnds: Knit.

Rnd 5: [K1, yo, knit to the next marked st, yo] 4 times—32 sts.

Repeat rnds 4 and 5 thirteen more times—136 sts: 1 corner st plus 33 sts in each section.

Lace panel one

Rnd 1: Knit.

Rnd 2: [K1, yo, *k2tog, yo; repeat from * to 1 st before marked st, k1, yo] 4 times—35 sts in each section.

Repeat rnds 1 and 2 of lace pattern once—37 sts in each section.

Rnd 3: Knit.

Rnd 4: [K1, yo, knit to the next marked st, yo] 4 times—39 sts in each section.

Repeat rnds 3 and 4 six more times—51 sts in each section.

Lace panel two

Rnd 1: Knit.

Rnd 2: [K1, yo, *k2tog, yo; repeat from * to 1 st before marked st, k1, yo] 4 times—53 sts in each section.

Repeat Rnds 1 and 2 two more times—57 sts in each section.

Rnd 3: Knit.

Rnd 4: [K1, yo, knit to the next marked st, yo] 4 times—59 sts in each section.

Repeat rnds 3 and 4 eight more times—75 sts in each section.

Lace panel three

Rnd 1: Knit.

Rnd 2: [K1, yo, *k2tog, yo; repeat from * to 1 st before marked st, k1, yo] 4 times—77 sts in each section.

Repeat rnds 1 and 2 three more times—83 sts in each section.

Rnd 3: Knit.

Rnd 4: [K1, yo, knit to the next marked st, yo] 4 times—85 sts in each section.

Repeat rnds 3 and 4 eleven more times—107 sts in each section.

Lace panel four

Rnd 1: Knit.

Rnd 2: [K1, yo, *k2tog, yo; repeat from * to 1 st before marked st, k1, yo] 4 times—109 sts in each section.

Repeat rnds 1 and 2 four more times—117 sts in each section.

Rnd 3: Knit.

Rnd 4: [K1, yo, knit to the next marked st, yo] 4 times—119 sts in each section.

Repeat rnds 3 and 4 fourteen more times—147 sts in each section.

Lace panel five

Rnd 1: Knit.

Rnd 2: [K1, yo, *k2tog, yo; repeat from * to 1 st before marked st, k1, yo] 4 times—149 sts in each section.

Repeat rnds 1 and 2 five more times—159 sts in each section.

Rnd 3: Knit.

Rnd 4: [K1, yo, knit to the next marked st, yo] 4 times—161 sts in each section.

Repeat rnds 3 and 4 seventeen more times—195 sts in each section.

Lace panel six

Rnd 1: Knit.

Rnd 2: [K1, yo, *k2tog, yo; repeat from * to 1 st before marked st, k1, yo] 4 times—197 sts in each section.

Repeat rnds 1 and 2 six more times—209 sts in each section.

Border

Rnd 1: Purl.

Rnd 2: *K1, yo, knit to next marker, yo; repeat from *—211 sts in each section.

Repeat rnds 1 and 2 once—213 sts in each section, 856 total sts.

Finishing

Bind off loosely. Use tapestry needle to weave in ends. Block.

Bibliography

Baerentsen, Elsa. *Foroysk Bindingarmynstur*. Torshavn: Foroyskt Heimavirki, 1983.

Carter, Hazel. *Shetland Lace Knitting from Charts*. Madison, Wisconsin: Hazel Carter,1987.

Don, Sarah. *The Art of Shetland Lace*. Berkeley, California: Lacis, 1991.

Glover, Medrith and Karen Yacsik. "The Graceful." *Knitters Magazine* #13, Winter 1988, Vol.5, No.4. Sioux Falls, South Dakota: Golden Fleece Publications, 1988.

Greenhowe, Jean. *Jean Greenhowe's Bazaar Knits*. Aberdeen, Scotland: Jean Greenhowe Designs, 1990.

Halldorsdottir, Sigridur. *Prihyrnur og Langsol*. Reykjavik, Iceland: Heimilisionaoarfelag Islands, 1988.

Ivantis, Linda J. *Russian Folk Belief*. New York: M. E. Sharpe, Inc., 1989.

Lewis, Susanna E. *Knitting Lace*. Newtown, Connecticut: Taunton Press, 1992.

Lind, Vibeke. *Knitting in the Nordic Tradition*. Asheville, North Carolina: Lark Books, 1984.

MacDonald, Anne L. *No Idle Hands: The Social History of American Knitting*. New York: Ballantine Books, 1988.

MacManus, Diarmuid. *Irish Earth Folk*. New York: The Devin-Adair Company, 1959.

McKie, Scott. *Women's Fancy Shawl Dancing*. Eau claire, Wisconsin: "News From Indian Country": The Nations Native Journal, Mid January 1998.

Pagoldh, Susanne. *Nordic Knitting*. Loveland, Colorado: Interweave Press, 1991.

Raczek, Thersa. *Rainy's Powwow*. Flagstaff, Arizona: Rising Moon, 1999.

Sayer, Chloe. *Mexican Patterns*. New York: Portland House, 1990.

Seto, T. *1000 Knitting Patterns Book*. Japan: Nihon Vogue, 1992.

Stanfield, Lesley. *The New Knitting Stitch Library*. Radnor, Pennsylvania: Chilton Book Company, 1992.

Toor, Frances. *A Treasury of Mexican Folkways*. New York: Crown Publishers, 1947.

Van Keppel, Marilyn. *Faroese Knitting Patterns*. Pittsville, Wisconsin: Schoolhouse Press, 1997.

Waddell, John, J. W. O'Connell, Anne Korff, editors. *The Book of Aran*. Galway: Tir Eolas, 1994.

Walker, Barbara G. *A Treasury of Knitting Patterns*. New York: Charles Schribner's Sons, 1968

——*A Second Treasury of Knitting Patterns*. New York: Charles Scribner's Sons, 1970

——*The Woman's Dictionary of Symbols & Sacred Objects*. San Francisco: Harper San Francisco, 1988.

——*The Woman's Encyclopedia of Myths and Secrets*. San Francisco: Harper and Row Publishers, 1983.

Waterman, Martha. *Traditional Knitted Lace Shawls*. Loveland, Colorado: Interweave Press, 1998.

Yamanaka, Norio. *The Book of Kimono*. Tokyo: Kodansha International Ltd., 1982.

Yarn Sources

Alice Starmore Scottish Campion
Unicorn Books and Crafts, 1338 Ross St., Petaluma, CA 94954, 800-289-9276.

Black Water Abbey Yarn
Blackwater Abbey Yarns, 22 South Albion, Suite 222, Denver, CO 80222, 303-756-2714.

Blackberry Ridge Woolen Mill Silk Blends
Blackberry Ridge Woolen Mill, 3776 Forshaug Rd., Mt. Horeb, WI 53572-1012, 608-437-3762.

Cashmere America 2-Ply
Cashmere America, PO Box 1126, Sonora, TX 76950, 915-387-6052.

Cheryl Oberle Designs Dancing Colors
Cheryl Oberle Designs, 3315 Newton Street, Denver, CO 80211, 303-433-9205.

Creative Yarns International Superkid Luxe
Creative Yarns International, 911 Western Ave., Suite 303, Seattle, WA 98104, 206-933-7344.

Harrisville Designs Shetland
Harrisville Designs, Box 806 Center Village, Harrisville, NH 03450, 603-827-3333, www.harrisville.com

Henry's Attic Cascade, Henry's Attic Monty
Henry's Attic, 5 Mercury Avenue, Monroe, NY 10950-3736, 914-783-3930.

Icelandic Laceweight Wool, Jamieson & Smith Shetland, Unspun Icelandic Wool
Schoolhouse Press, 6899 Cary Bluff, Pittsville, WI 54466, 715-884-2799

Nature Spun Sport
Brown Sheep Company, Rte 1, Mitchell, NE 69357, 308-635-2198.

Tahki Cotton Classic
Tahki Yarns, 11 Graphic Place, Moonachie, NJ 07074, 201-807-0070, www.tahki.com.

Wool Pak Yarn N.Z.
Baabajoes Wool Company, PO Box 260604, Lakewood, CO 80226, www.baabajoeswool.com.

Index

MORE FOLK TITLES FROM INTERWEAVE PRESS

Folk Knitting in Estonia: A Garland of Symbolism, Tradition, and Technique

Nancy Bush

Folk Knitting in Estonia explores the fascinating history of the craft and the country. You will find clearly illustrated, step-by-step instructions for 26 gloves, mittens, and socks, both historic and contemporary, using traditional patterns typical of Estonian knitting.

8½ × 9, paperbound, 120 pages, color and b&w photos, line drawings and charts. #795—$21.95/$32.95 CAN

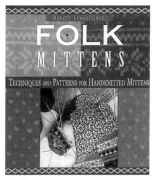

Folk Mittens: Techniques and Patterns for Handknitted Mittens

Marcia Lewandowski

Folk Mittens offers 38 mitten patterns from around the world, presented with full-color charts and photographs. Following an introduction to folk knitting, there is a section on techniques for knitting mittens. The author also provides techniques for handknitted mitten cords, sizing, and finishing. Each mitten captures the spirit of the culture from which it comes.

8½ × 9, paperbound, 120 pages, 38 charts and patterns. #694—$18.95/$28.95 CAN

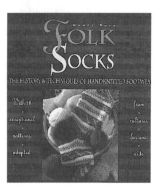

Folk Socks: The History and Techniques of Handknitted Footwear

Nancy Bush

Nancy Bush has culled museum archives in Europe and the British Isles to present 18 great sock patterns from a host of folk knitting traditions. *Folk Socks* includes careful directions, charts, and illustrations, in addition to a chapter on techniques. There's also a collection of heel turnings, toe shapings, and top ribbings for knitters at all levels of experience.

8½ × 9, paperbound, 120 pages, color and b&w photos, line drawings and charts. #654—$18.95/$28.95 CAN

800-272-2193
www.interweave.com